# Approaching Music Notation

Music notation is a language and, as such, it must be communicable. The closer the notation adheres to common rules and guidelines, the more successfully the music will be performed. The rules and guidelines presented here will make the notation easier to read and will help to make the musical intent clear. Although these rules are not inflexible, they should not be ignored.

For music notation, the first priority is always clarity. Choices need to be made that are solely dependent on the situation; a rule may not provide the most desirable answer to a problem. (It would be an endless task to list every musical exception to a rule.) Problems are usually solved by deciding which rule is more flexible (least important to clarity).

Although meticulous adjustment can only clarify and beautify the notation, sometimes such attention to detail is not practical. All decisions must depend on a wide variety of situations. An understanding of the rules allows these choices to be made wisely—the notation can only be as good as the knowledge at hand.

# About This Book

The Essential Dictionary of Music Notation is in an easy-to-use format, which includes cross referencing. At the top of each page, running heads show exactly which topic is being treated on that page. Bold treatments of text highlight important points for clarity and quick reference.

Text is accompanied by numerous examples directly related to the topic being discussed. These examples are kept as simple and complete as possible, with an emphasis on presenting correct and current notation practices. Obsolete rules are mentioned only when necessary.

The focus of this book has been narrowed, avoiding the discussion of orchestration or music theory, in order to present as much information as possible that is directly related to the actual notation of music. The serious musician is encouraged to seek out other sources that more thoroughly address the subjects of orchestration and music theory.

Whether you are using a pencil or a computer, all principles within this book are applicable. No computer software or specific tool is referenced, in order to make this a useful guide for any musician.

An Index of Topics is provided on the last page.

# Essential Dictionary
## of
# MUSIC
# NOTATION

The most practical and concise source for music notation

## TOM GEROU
## LINDA LUSK

Alfred Publishing Co., Inc.
Los Angeles

Library of Congress Cataloging–in–Publication Data

Gerou, Tom
Essential dictionary of music notation: the most practical and concise
source for music notation / Tom Gerou, Linda Lusk.  p. cm.
ISBN: 0-88284-730-9 (alk. paper)
1. Musical notation—Dictionaries.  2. Music printing—Dictionaries.  I.
Lusk, Linda.  II. Title.
MT35.G494 1996
780'.148—dc20    96—32544
CIP
MN

*Thanks to Morty & Iris Manus, Don Ferguson,*
*Christopher Marella and James & Florence Gerou*

Cover design:  Carol Kascsak/Ted Engelbart
Interior design:  Tom Gerou
Interior production:  Tom Gerou, Linda Lusk

Cover art, center photo:  From an Antiphoner,
or book of music for the choir services.
Copyright © Sotheby's
Circuitry photo: © PhotoDisc, Inc.

# A *cappella*

Vocal music that is to be sung **without accompaniment** (a cappella) often has a piano part for rehearsal only.

> The piano part may be full size or cue size (see *Cue notes*). If cue size, the staff should be cue size also. (Cue-size notes on a full-size staff are not as easy to read.)

> The indication *for rehearsal only* should be clearly placed above the piano part.

# A *due (a2)*        See Sharing a staff

# A *tempo*

Place above the staff (sometimes within the grand staff) to indicate a return to the normal tempo. Used after tempo alterations such as *ritardando, accelerando, più lento* or *ad libitum.*   (See *Tempo marks*)

# Accents        See Articulations

# *Accidentals*

Temporary alterations to the pitch of a note.

## THE 5 SYMBOLS

If appearing in the music, apart from use in the key signature, these symbols are called *accidentals*.

♯    **Sharp**
Raises a note one half step.

🗙    **Double-sharp**
Raises a note two half steps.

♭    **Flat**
Lowers a note one half step.

♭♭    **Double-flat**
Lowers a note two half steps.    Notice that the flats touch, forming one symbol.

♮    **Natural**
Cancels any of the above, whether indicated in the key signature or as an accidental.

# ONE ACCIDENTAL PER NOTE

**Do not use multiple accidentals** on one note. (A double-flat is a single accidental.)

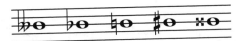

*Accidentals shown altering one note
from lowest to highest.*

The lowest a note can be lowered is a ♭♭.

The highest a note can be raised is a 𝄪.

# WITHIN A MEASURE

Any accidental is **cancelled when a new accidental appears** on the like pitch.

*Notice that only the flat (not ♮♭) is needed to change
from a double-flat to a flat.*

An accidental affects all **subsequent notes of the same pitch** within the measure.

An accidental **must be added again** in the following measure.

An accidental **carries over to a tied note**
extending from one measure to the next.

The accidental will reappear only
when the note is re-struck.

*add accidental again*

*no repeat of accidental*

## OCTAVE ALTERATIONS

Accidentals **do not apply if an *8va* sign is**
added; repeat the accidentals.

## COURTESY ACCIDENTALS

Used as **reminders of the key signature** when an accidental has been used in the previous measure, or to **avoid ambiguity** in certain situations.

Use a courtesy accidental as a **reminder** to return to the original pitch.

*courtesy accidental*

Courtesy accidentals may or may not be enclosed in **parentheses.** The parentheses show that it *is* a courtesy accidental, and help avoid confusion about the key signature. However, if many courtesy accidentals are used, and the piece is also crowded, the parentheses could make it look cluttered and more complicated. For this reason some editors choose not to use parentheses at all.

If a chord has more than one courtesy accidental, **each accidental gets its own pair of parentheses.**

It is best to **add a courtesy accidental for octave shifts** although the notes of the same pitch in different octaves are considered separately.

*courtesy accidental for clarity*

*accidental applies to this note only*

## GRACE NOTES WITH ACCIDENTALS

The accidental placed on a grace note will be smaller (cue size), like the grace note.

The accidental **affects all subsequent notes of the same pitch** within the measure.

Depending on the clarity of the situation, **courtesy accidentals are often needed** to avoid confusion.

*grace-note accidental applies to entire measure, yet...*

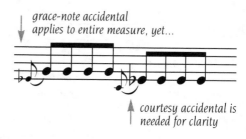

*courtesy accidental is needed for clarity*

## ALIGNMENT FOR INTERVALS (2 Notes)

For intervals of a **2nd through a 6th,** place the upper accidental closest to the note, the lower accidental to the left.

When intervals are **greater than a 6th,** accidentals align vertically.

For the **interval of a 6th,** if the two accidentals don't collide they may be aligned vertically.

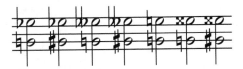

## ALIGNMENT FOR CHORDS (3 Notes)

When outer notes are a **6th or less,** the upper accidental is closest to the note, the lower accidental is placed left, and the middle accidental is placed farthest left.

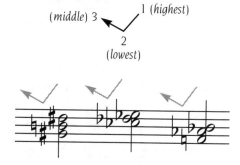

When outer notes are **greater than a 6th,** upper and lower accidentals are aligned closest to the notes—the middle accidental is placed to the left.

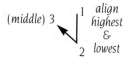

## ALIGNMENT FOR CHORDS
(More than 3 Notes)

> When dealing with accidentals for complex chords, rules are treated more as guidelines or suggestions. Keep the arrangement of the accidentals as compact as possible.

Make the arrangement of accidentals as **easy to read as possible** for the situation.

> **Align the highest and lowest** accidentals whenever possible.
>
> The **center accidentals are usually arranged diagonally** from highest to lowest.
>
> **Align accidentals for octaves** whenever possible.

**Accidentals for the 2nd** should usually be **shaped like the 2nd** (if the outer notes are greater than a 6th).

The upper accidental is placed closest to the note, the lower accidental to the left.

**Accidentals are always placed before** the entire note structure. (Do not place an accidental between notes that are played together, even if they are stemmed in opposite direction.)

## TWO PARTS ON A STAFF

For multiple notes played by **one instrument,** an accidental carries through the measure. Cancellations must be applied.

*one instrument—*
*the accidentals carry through the measure*

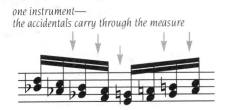

Parts on the same staff that are played by **more than one instrument** (including vocal parts) are treated individually. Repeat accidentals in the same measure if the voices cross.

*two instruments sharing a staff—*
*the accidentals are considered separately*

*courtesy accidental*
*avoids confusion*

## CHROMATIC PASSAGES

In general, use **sharps when ascending, flats when descending.**

When choosing accidentals, consider the context of the music, such as key signature, harmony and voice leading.

In the chord below, both a sharp and a flat are required (C♯, not D♭; E♭ not D♯).

*augmented 6th chord*

## ACCIDENTALS WITH TRILLS　　(See *Trill*)

## ACCIDENTALS IN HARP MUSIC

(See *Pedal marks*)

# Alternating instruments

## CONCERT ORCHESTRA / BAND

1. To alternate instruments, enough **time must be given** to allow the change.

2. During the measures of rest the indication *"Muta in [second instrument]"* is indicated **below** the staff as soon as the first instrument stops.

3. Any change to the **key signature** occurs after the barline following the rest, before the new instrument begins.

4. The **new instrument is indicated** above the entrance of the instrument.

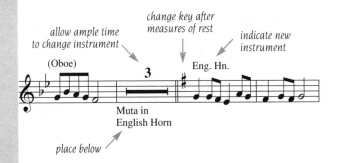

*allow ample time to change instrument*

*change key after measures of rest*

*indicate new instrument*

(Oboe)

**3**

Eng. Hn.

Muta in
English Horn

*place below*

## INCORPORATING CUES

1. Cue notes should be **added after many measures of rest,** to help the performer make a correct entrance.

2. The cued instrument is **indicated above the passage** in a smaller type size.

3. The **key signature changes at the beginning** of the cue.

4. **Full-size rests** are indicated below (or above, depending on stem direction).

(See *Cue notes*)

## JAZZ ENSEMBLE

All rules above apply except that "muta in
[...]" is written **"Change to [new
instrument]"** and is placed **above** the staff.

*for jazz orchestra
place above staff*

(Alto Sax)     Change to Flute     Fl.

## COMMONLY ALTERNATING INSTRUMENTS

The following is a listing of commonly
alternating instruments in a standard
orchestra:

|              | *Alternate*      |
| ------------ | ---------------- |
| Flute III    | Piccolo          |
| Oboe III     | English horn     |
| Clarinet III | Bass clarinet    |
| Bassoon III  | Contrabassoon    |

*In smaller orchestras, the second player
alternates in all cases above.*

# *Arpeggio signs*

A vertical wavy line before a chord or interval indicates an arpeggio (rolled chord).

## ARPEGGIO DIRECTION

The chord is to be played quickly from **bottom to top** (no direction arrow).

*played upward*
*(no direction arrow)*

If the arpeggio is to be played from **top to bottom, an arrowhead is added** to the bottom of the wavy line.

*played downward*

**When the arpeggio returns to normal**
(bottom to top) or alternates with an
arpeggio played downward, an arrowhead
is added to the top of the wavy line.

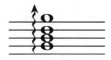

*played upward*

The arpeggio sign **should not extend
much past the chord** affected.

## PLACEMENT WITH ACCIDENTALS

Arpeggio signs are always **placed before
accidentals**.

*allow space
for accidentals*

## FOR KEYBOARD INSTRUMENTS
## AND HARP

The arpeggio sign **can extend across both staves.** The right hand begins after the left hand has completed the chord.

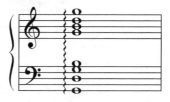

*played upward,
from bottom to top*

**If the wavy line is broken** between staves, both hands begin the arpeggio simultaneously.

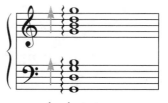

*hands start
simultaneously*

## FOR HARP

**Use an arpeggio sign only** if an arpeggio is *clearly* wanted since harpists naturally tend to roll all chords.

**A bracket can be added** if chords are *not* to be arpeggiated.

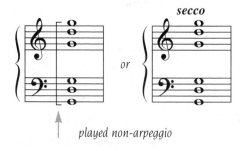

*or*

*played non-arpeggio*

The term ***secco***, or ***dry sec***, may be used instead of the bracket.

# Articulations

Articulations are symbols used to indicate *how* a note or chord is played, alone or in relation to other notes and chords.

There are five main articulations: **staccatissimo, staccato, tenuto, accent, marcato.**

An articulation's **influence on a note or chord varies** depending on its context. A staccato note in a slower tempo is not played as short as it would be played in a faster tempo. An accent is softer in the dynamic *p* than in the dynamic *f*.

**One articulation applies to all** notes of an interval or chord (on one stem).

## DURATIONAL ARTICULATIONS

There are three articulations that **affect the duration** of a note or chord: *staccatissimo* ( ᵛ ), *staccato* (·) and *tenuto* (–).

*The following illustrates durational articulations compared to an unmarked note, from shortest to longest.*

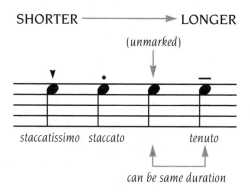

## Staccatissimo

The shape varies slightly among engravers, but is always wedge-shaped. It indicates that a note or chord is to be played as **short as possible.**

*staccatissimo*

Used only with note values of a quarter note or less.

The *staccatissimo* is **centered on the notehead**. Placement is in the next space from the notehead, whether the note is on a line or space.

**Center on the stem** for opposite stem direction.

## Staccato

A dot above or below a note or chord indicates that the note or chord is to be played **short.**

*staccato*

Used with note values of a quarter note or less.

The *staccato* is **centered on the notehead**. Placement is in the next space from the notehead, whether the note is on a line or space.

**Center on the stem** for opposite stem direction.

## Tenuto

A short, heavy line above or below a note or chord, **thicker than the staff lines.**

A tenuto indicates that a note or chord is to be **held for its full value** (durational articulation), or the intent may be to apply a **slight stress** (articulation of force).

*tenuto*

However it is interpreted, the tenuto is meant to ensure that a note or chord will be given a **certain amount of attention.**

This emphasis allows the tenuto to be **flexible in its application,** especially when combined with other articulations.

The tenuto is sometimes referred to as a *sostenuto* or *stress*.

Used with notes of any rhythmic value.

The *tenuto* is **centered on the notehead**. Placement is in the next space from the notehead, whether the note is on a line or space.

Also **center to the notehead,** not the stem, for **opposite stem direction.**

## ARTICULATIONS OF FORCE

There are three articulations that affect the **force of attack** of a note or chord: the *tenuto* [–] discussed earlier, *accent* [>] and *marcato* [Λ].*

*The following illustrates articulations of force compared to an unmarked note, from lesser to greater force of attack.*

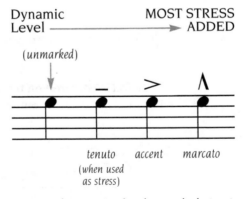

Dynamic Level ⟶ MOST STRESS ADDED

(*unmarked*)

tenuto (*when used as stress*)    accent    marcato

*Terminology varies for the symbols [ > ] and [ Λ ]. For the sake of this discussion, the words *accent* and *marcato* have been attached to the symbols.

## Accent

When an *accent* is placed over or under a note or chord, the note or chord is to be played with **more attack, more marked.**

Used with notes of any rhythmic value.

The *accent* is **centered on the notehead.** Preferred placement is **outside the staff.**

Although it is to be avoided, sometimes placing an accent **within the staff** is acceptable. A decision needs to be made whether it is preferred to have the accent closer to the notehead, or outside the staff.

**Center to the notehead,** not the stem, for **opposite stem direction.**

## Marcato

When the *marcato* is placed over or under a note or chord, the note or chord is to be played with **even more attack, and more marked,** than an *accent*.

marcato

Used with notes of any rhythmic value.

The *marcato* is **centered on the notehead.** Preferred placement is **outside the staff** and ***above*** the staff.

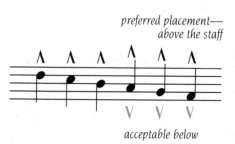

*preferred placement— above the staff*

*acceptable below*

Also **center to the notehead** (not the stem) for **opposite stem direction**.

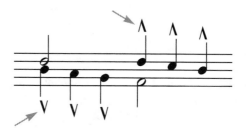

## OTHER ARTICULATIONS OF FORCE

*Sforzando* (**sf**), *forzando/forzato* (**fz**) and *sforzato* (**sfz**) are also included in this articulation group and are interchangeable with accents and marcato accents, depending on the dynamic range.

These three articulations have the benefit of a built-in **indicator of dynamics**.

*For instance, a* **sf** *should be indicated only in the dynamic ranges from* **ppp** *to* **f**. *With each increase of dynamic level, the sforzando reflects the higher dynamic level:* **sff** *in* **ff**, **sfff** *in* **fff**.

The following chart illustrates the relationships between *accent* [>] and *marcato* [Λ] to *sforzando* [**sf**], *forzando* [**fz**], and *sforzato* [**sfz**] within various dynamic levels.

### Dynamic Range

| + | *ppp* to *f* | *ff* | *fff* |
|---|---|---|---|
| > | s*f* | s*ff* | s*fff* |
| Λ | *fz* | *ffz* | *fffz* |
| <u>Λ</u> | s*fz* | s*ffz* | s*fffz* |

A [>] in *f* is comparable to a [s*f*].
A [<u>Λ</u>] in *fff* is comparable to a [s*fffz*].

## COMBINED ARTICULATIONS

Durational articulations can be combined with articulations of force to create variations of the basic articulations.

*The following examples are the most used combinations.*

**Staccatissimo** and **staccato** are never combined (they basically have the same function in varying degrees).

**Accent** and **marcato** are never combined for the same reason.

**Staccatissimo** and **tenuto** are not commonly combined.

**Staccatissimo** and **marcato** are not commonly combined.

## Combining articulations with tenuto

The **dual function** of the tenuto—the idea of *more importance, more attention*, whether of duration or force (or both)—allows the tenuto to be combined with either articulation group.

When a tenuto is **combined with an articulation of force,** the tenuto has more of a *durational function*, but may also retain its idea of force.

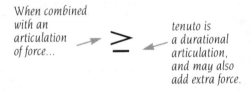

When *combined with an articulation of force...*

*tenuto is a durational articulation, and may also add extra force.*

When a tenuto is **combined with a durational articulation,** the tenuto has the function of an *articulation of force*, while retaining its durational function.

Tenuto is an articulation
of force
and                          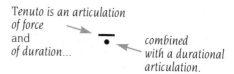          combined
of duration...                                            with a durational
                                                          articulation.

Usual interpretation:  play detached and
                       with a slight stress.

## PLACEMENT WHEN COMBINED

The following can be used as guides for the
placement of combined articulations:

*tenuto & staccato*

*accent & staccato*

*marcato & staccato*

**Keep the two combined articulations together** (on the same side of the note) whenever possible.

Notice that when a **staccato** is combined with another articulation (and is on the same side of the note), it is **centered on the notehead,** even when it is on the stem side.

## SIMILE

When an articulation (or pattern of articulations) is applied in a repetitious and predictable manner, the word *simile* may be used.

> *Simile* is indicated **after the pattern has been clearly established** (usually two or three measures).

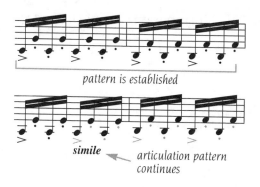

*pattern is established*

*simile* ← *articulation pattern continues*

Notice that the *simile* was **not used at the beginning of the line,** even though the pattern had already been established.

The **simile** is ended when the pattern ends or when different articulations are added.

(articulations continue)                    simile stops

## SLURS WITH ARTICULATIONS    (See Slurs)

# Attacca

**Attacca** or **attacca subito** means to proceed immediately to the next movement without a break.    (See Volti subito)

> **Attacca** is placed below (and at the end of) the last measure of the movement.
>
> **Segue** is sometimes used instead of **attacca.**

# *Augmentation dot*

### PLACEMENT

Always place **one dot per space** and **only in a space**—never on a staff line or on the same level as a leger line.

> **For a line note**—place to the right of the notehead, **in the space above.**

> **For a space note**—place to the right of the notehead **in the same space** as the note.

**For notes with a flag**—the dot is placed further right, altogether **avoiding the flag.** Never place a dot between the notehead and its flag.

**Double and triple dots** are placed directly to the right of the first dot. Horizontal spacing is equal to that of the first dot. *Multiple dots should be used only in situations where they will be easily understood.*

**Never separate a dot from its notehead.**
Stem direction and creative positioning of
a dotted note must be considered.

**Ties always avoid the dot**—place the tie
clearly to the right of the dot.

For two or more notes in a chord with the
same stem direction, **always align the
dots vertically.**

**Two dots never share the same space.**

## FOR INTERVALS OF A SECOND

The dot for the space note is always placed in the space to the right of the notehead.

If the **line note is above,** place the dot in the space above. If the **line note is below,** place the dot in the space below.

## FOR TWO OR MORE PARTS

**For stems up,** place dots for line notes in the space above. **For stems down,** place in the space below.

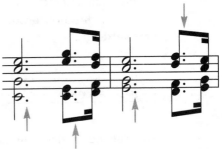

## DOTTED RESTS

Rests are dotted in the same way notes are dotted, but with some restrictions on their use.

Place the dots as follows:

Dotted rests are used mainly to **clarify the subdivision of a measure.**   (See Meter)

> **Dotted whole rests** are the least used of all the dotted rests.  They are never used in simple meter.
>
> *Possible use of dotted whole rest:*

Likewise, **a dotted half rest** should not be used in simple meter.

*Possible uses of dotted half rest:*

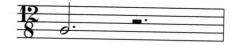

**Dotted quarter rests** are used in compound meters. Avoid using them in simple meters.

In $\frac{6}{8}$ time, dotted quarter rests can be used on beats 1 and 4 only.

In $\frac{9}{8}$ time, dotted quarter rests can be
used on beats 1, 4 and 7 only (the pulses).

In $\frac{12}{8}$ time, do NOT use a dotted half rest
across the middle of the measure.  Use
dotted quarter rests.

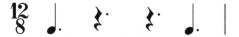

It is acceptable to use the **dotted eighth
rest, dotted sixteenth rest, etc.,** for a
cleaner look.

# *Barlines*

Barlines are vertical lines that divide a staff into measures.

## SINGLE BARLINE

The **thickness of a barline** is equal to, or greater than, the staff line thickness (staff lines being thicker than stems).

To help the performer follow the music from staff to staff, **avoid the alignment of barlines** from staff to staff (or from system to system).

**Allow a small amount of space after** a barline—depending upon the density of notes within the measure.

*normal space after barline*

**Less space** may be allowed **after** the barline if the **density of notes is high.**

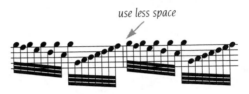

**More space** may be allowed **after** the barline if the **density of notes is low.**

**Less space** may be allowed **before** the barline if **density is high.** Avoid *adding* space before the barline.

If there is no other rhythm in any other voice, allow **more space** after the barline for a whole note (or any note having the value of a whole measure).

## DOUBLE BARLINE (Thin/thin)

**Used to clarify the end of a section** of music, such as in a *Da Capo* layout.

*D.C. al Fine*

## FINAL DOUBLE BARLINE (Thin/thick)

Marks the **end of a composition, or the end of a movement** within a larger work.

Consists of a thin barline followed by a thick barline.

## BROKEN BARLINES

Broken (dashed) barlines are sometimes used when a situation calls for the completion of a section **mid-measure,** although the **final double barline** is preferred.

For composite meters, a broken barline is sometimes used to **clarify the meter division** within a measure.

### THE LEFT BARLINE

A single staff should ***never* begin** with a barline.

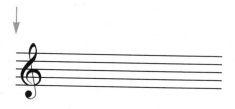

### SYSTEMIC BARLINE

A systemic barline connects two or more staves together, as in the grand staff.

Barlines are **used to group staves of like instruments** in a score layout.

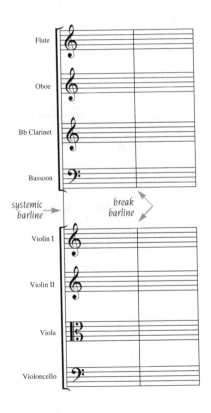

## WITH CHANGING CLEFS

The new clef (cue size) is placed **before the barline** if the clef changes mid-staff.

*new clef placed
before the barline
mid-staff* ↓

A **courtesy clef is placed before the last barline** of the staff if the new clef begins immediately on the next staff.

*courtesy clef placed
before the barline,
end of staff* ↓

(See *Clef signs*)

## WITH CHANGING KEY SIGNATURES

The new key signature is **placed after** an added **double barline** if the key signature changes mid-staff.

*new key signature placed after the barline mid-staff*

A **courtesy** key signature is **placed after** the last barline (add double bar) if the new key signature begins on the following staff.

*courtesy key signature placed after the barline*

*leave open*

**Note:** *A single barline may be used in both the above instances, but a double bar calls more attention to the change.*

# WITH CHANGING TIME SIGNATURES

The time signature is **placed after** the bar-line if the time signature changes mid-staff.

*time signature placed
after the barline
mid-staff* ↓

A **courtesy** time signature is **placed after** the last barline if the new time signature begins on the following staff.

*courtesy time signature* ↓
*placed after the barline* →

*leave open* ↑

## WITH MULTIPLE COURTESY SIGNS

If a courtesy clef, key signature and time signature all appear together, they follow the rules for each individual courtesy change.

**The order is the same** as the order presented at the beginning of the piece (clef, key signature, time signature).

## INCOMPLETE MEASURES

If a piece begins with a **pick-up,** the barline is positioned **according to the time value of the beat(s).**

# Beams

Although sometimes referred to as "balkans" or "ligatures," **"beam"** is the preferred term for the connection between two or more consecutive notes, replacing the flag.

> Beams greatly simplify the reading of music, **substituting for individual flags** in groupings of **notes smaller than a quarter note.**
>
> Because of the **ease in reading of beams,** the **use of flags in vocal music**—in relation to the lyric—has become **obsolete.**

## CONNECTION TO THE STEM

Beams are connected to the side of the stem. They must be **flush to the stem,** both vertically and horizontally.

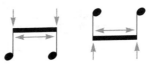

## PRIMARY AND SECONDARY BEAMS

The beam that is furthest from the noteheads and connects a group of notes is called a *primary beam*. This beam **remains unbroken** throughout the grouping.

Any beam other than the primary beam is a *secondary beam*. The secondary beam **may be broken,** to divide the grouping into smaller units for easier reading.

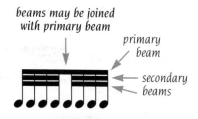

**Stems extend through secondary beams** and connect to the primary beam.

## DOUBLE BEAMS

**Normal stem length** will accommodate a double beam—the stem need not be adjusted.

## TRIPLE AND QUADRUPLE BEAMS

When a third or fourth beam is added below the secondary beam, **the stems must be extended** by approximately one staff space per beam.

The extension of the stems allows the space between the noteheads and the lowest beam to remain normal.

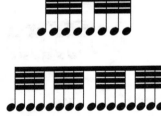

*If 32nd- and 64th-note values occupy the majority of the rhythmic values, it may be better to double the rhythmic values of the entire piece and alter the tempo.*

## FRACTIONAL BEAMS

A fractional beam is also a **secondary beam.**

Fractional beams are **associated with only one note.**

The **length** of a fractional beam is the same as the width of a notehead.

**Place** exactly the same as a full-length secondary beam would be placed. The beam is always *inside* the grouping, and it usually follows or precedes a beamed dotted note.

## BEAMING AND METER

The basic purpose of beaming is to **connect two or more notes within the same beat (or pulse).** Meter must be considered when grouping notes with a beam.    (See Meter)

In **any simple meter,** each beat is divisible by two; a beam may connect the two notes. Simple duple, simple triple and simple quadruple meters each have slightly different considerations.

### Simple duple meter ($\frac{2}{2}$, $\frac{2}{4}$, $\frac{2}{8}$)

In some cases, the entire measure may be beamed.

*Some combinations of beams, flags and rests in simple duple meter:*

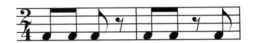

Although some contemporary engravers beam over a rest at the beginning or ending of a beamed grouping 𝄽♩𝄽♩ , it is not the preferred notation.

## Simple triple meter ($\frac{3}{2}$, $\frac{3}{4}$, $\frac{3}{8}$)

Consideration is given to **visually maintain** the three beats within the measure. In some cases the entire measure may be beamed.

*or*

It is better to **avoid arbitrary groupings** of 4+2 or 2+4. However, they are sometimes used to emphasize phrasing.

The combined use of **flags and beams** clarify the meter.

Avoid beaming in a manner that would suggest ⅜ time. Use flagged notes to differentiate ¾ meter from ⅜ meter.

*use flagged notes to avoid groupings of three*

**Beaming to include rests** inside the grouping is acceptable.

## Simple quadruple meter ($\frac{4}{4}$, $\frac{4}{8}$)

In $\frac{4}{4}$ time, beats 1 & 2 and beats 3 & 4 may be beamed together to form a unit.

*Never connect the notes of beat 2 with beat 3.*

The basic rule in $\frac{4}{4}$ time is that the **two halves** of the measure (beats 1 & 3) **must be immediately recognizable.** The only exception to this would be a very simple syncopation (such as ♩♩♩).

Because of this rule, all the notes in the measure would *not* be beamed together, as is possible in the other simple meters.

*or*

THE SAME RHYTHM THREE WAYS
Each could be the best for a particular
situation.

Notice that **each beat** is recognizable in
the following example.

Notated with beams only, the **two halves**
of the measure are easily recognizable:

If the above example were in a piece that
contained triplets, it could at first glance
be **mistaken for triplets.** In that case, a
better notation would be:

For any simple meter, **when a beat is uneven or contains more than two notes,** the two adjacent beats should not be beamed together as a unit.

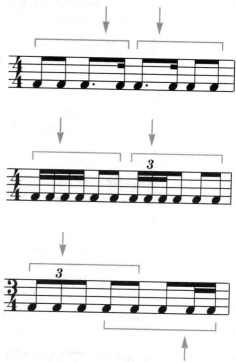

## Compound meter

When each **pulse** of the measure is
**divided into three beats,** the meter is
called "compound."  A beam may connect
the three beats.

*compound duple (2 pulses, 6 beats)*

*compound triple (3 pulses, 9 beats)*

*compound quadruple (4 pulses, 12 beats)*

The **units** of three beats **for each pulse** in compound meter **must always be maintained.** Even when rests are included in the measure, as in the example below, beats 1, 4 & 7 must be clearly visible.

*The three units in the above example could be made even more obvious by including the rest on beat 5 in a beamed unit.*

It is **possible to group all notes within a pulse.** All the notes in the *measure*, however, cannot be beamed together—this could cause the measure to appear to be in some other meter.

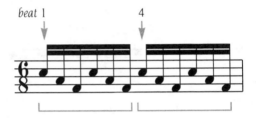

*Although different groupings are sometimes used for phrasing or interpretation, the above should be generally adhered to.*

## TIES AND BEAMS

Avoid using tied notes *within* a beamed grouping. The **unit should be broken** where the tie is placed.

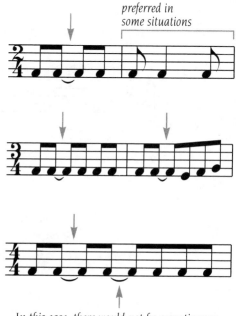

In this case, there would not be a continuous beam, since beats 2 and 3 should not be beamed together in this meter.

## STEM DIRECTION OF BEAMED GROUPS

Simple rules for stemming of single notes apply to beamed groups when possible (for example, if all notes in a beamed grouping are on or above the middle line of the staff, stems are down), but some additional guidelines are needed.          (See *Stems*)

### For two beamed notes

Stem direction is **determined by the note farther from the middle staff line.**

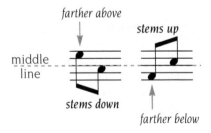

If both notes are **the same distance** from the middle line, the preference is for **stems down.**

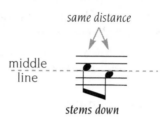

*same distance*

middle
line

*stems down*

If all other stems in the surrounding measures are up-stem, that direction is sometimes continued if the two notes are the same distance from the middle line. (This is a very subtle point, and somewhat obsolete.)

## For three or more beamed notes

If the majority of the notes are **on or above** the middle line, the stems go down.

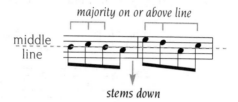

*majority on or above line*

middle line

*stems down*

If the majority of the notes are **below** the middle line, the stems are up.

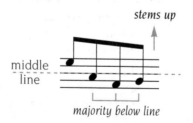

*stems up*

middle line

*majority below line*

If the number of notes **above and below the middle line are equal,** the note farthest from the middle line dictates the stem direction. (If all notes are the same distance, the preference is down.)

*farthest from middle*

*equal distance above and below line*

middle line

## BEAM SLANT & PLACEMENT
### Concerning the computer

With most computer engraving today, the direction, slant and placement of the beam are automatic.

However, the defaults—or even the settings allowable—may not conform to traditional practices. Even though some of these practices are in the process of change, there are some guidelines to keep in mind for a more professional look.

## Beginning placement of the beam

When **stems are up,** the stem length of the **highest note** determines the beam placement.

When **stems are down,** the stem length of the **lowest note** determines the beam placement.

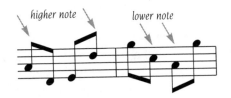

## Direction of slant

Beams *usually* **follow the contour of the notes,** ascending or descending.

For mixed direction of notes, the beam *usually* **follows the direction between the first and last note** of a grouping.

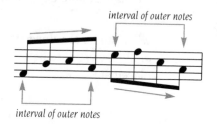

*interval of outer notes*

*interval of outer notes*

When two or more notes share a stem, the note **closest to the beam** dictates the beam direction.

## Horizontal beaming

A beam should be horizontal if the first and last note of the beamed group is on the **same pitch level**.

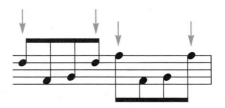

If the grouping consists of **repeated intervals,** the beam should be horizontal.

Horizontal beams may be used if inner notes **do not follow the interval direction** of the outer notes.

Some other examples of horizontal beaming:

## Interval-specific beam slant

Determining the placement and slant of beams in traditional plate engraving was complicated and detailed.

The following are *approximate* guidelines, **modified from the strict traditional** rules for beaming of intervals. There are two main reasons for this modification:

1. The consistency of the computer and the quality of modern printing make it no longer necessary to avoid the small "wedges" of white space that in the past often filled in with ink.

2. Adjusting many beams individually on the computer is very time-consuming.

A pair of **notes of different pitch should not have a horizontal beam.** (Exception: two notes on the same line or space, one or both altered with an accidental)

If a **beam slants, it is usually from 1/2 to 2 staff spaces**—very seldom more.

Intervals of a **2nd** slant 1/2 space.

*2nds*

Intervals of a **3rd** slant 1 staff space.

Intervals of a **4th** slant from 1 to 1-1/2 staff spaces.

Intervals of a **5th, 6th & 7th** each slant approximately 1 to 1-1/2 staff spaces.

*7ths*

Intervals of an **octave and greater** slant
1-1/2 to 2 staff spaces.

*octaves*

Beamed notes with **leger lines** slant 1/2
staff space. (Remember that stems must
extend to the middle line.)

*with leger lines*

Depending upon the **amount of space** allowed between the beamed notes, the slant of the beam naturally *decreases* with an *increase* in the amount of space allotted, if stem lengths remain the same.

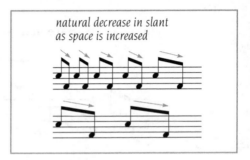

natural decrease in slant
as space is increased

For tightly spaced beamed notes, **adjust the slant** (by lengthening the stem of the farthest note) so that it is not so extreme.

becomes

## Alternative beaming

For grand staff notation, **cross-staff beaming** is acceptable in some situations. The slant of the beam is determined by the amount of space between the two staves, the length of the stems, and by avoiding exaggerated angles.

For single-staff music, alternative beaming should be used only in **exceptional circumstances.** Stems must not be too short.

# Bowing

**Down-bow** and **up-bow** markings are centered to the notehead and are placed above the staff, except when two parts share a staff.

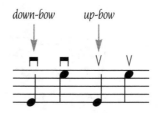

String techniques such as **spiccato, legato, portato** and **jeté** are notated conventionally, with slurs and/or articulations.

*The study of orchestration is necessary to properly specify string indications.*

**Slurs** can indicate either phrasing or bowing, or both.

Slurs can only partially indicate phrasing.

Notes within a **legato slur** are usually grouped under one bow-stroke. The bowing can change direction with the next slur.

If two slurs are indicated, both may be phrasing slurs, or a combination of phrasing and bowing.

If a particular bowing is desired, [⊓] or [∨] should be used.

If a particular technique is wanted, it is best to indicate it above the staff.

**Bariolage** is the alternation of an open string with a lower, fingered string. The open string is indicated with an 'o'.

Brackets to the left of the chord may be used for **multiple stops** if the chord is to be divided a particular way. Usually no bracket is used.

Multiple stops may be *double, triple* or *quadruple* stops.

A notehead is placed on both sides of the stem when **two strings are played in unison.**

The alternative notation uses **opposite stem direction.** The open string indication (**o**) is added for clarity.

This double-stop effect is **only possible on the top three strings** of each instrument.

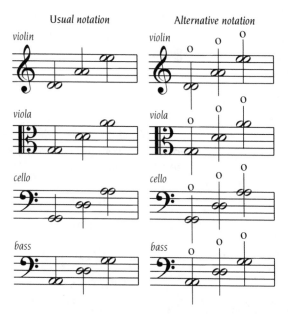

Usual notation      Alternative notation

## PLACEMENT OF TEXT

All text for bowing indications is **placed above** the staff.

When a particular string is to be played exclusively, *sul* [string] is indicated.

### *sul G*

*Pizzicato* is cancelled with the *arco* indication.

*pizz.*                    *arco*

With any of the following indications, *ord.* or *ordinario* is commonly used to indicate the return to normal playing.

### *non vib.*

### *sul pont.*

### *sul tasto*

### *col legno*

# Brace

The brace is used to connect the two staves in scores for instruments such as piano, organ, harp and marimba.

The brace connects two staves to form a **grand staff.**

The brace can **be extended to include three staves** in piano scores. Usually it is based on multi-levels in a composition too dense for clarity on two staves. (To be avoided—see next example.)

Most situations can be accommodated on two staves; more than two staves is rare.

# Bracket

The bracket is used **to connect two or more staves** to form a system or to **group certain instruments** within a system.

The bracket is different from the brace in that it connects the staves for two or more **separate instruments,** while the brace connects staves for one instrument (such as keyboard).

The grouping may be two or more **unlike** instruments, **identical** instruments, or a **family** of instruments, such as strings.

*connects unlike instruments*

*connects identical instruments*

Flute I

Flute II

*connects a family of instruments*

Violin I

Violin II

Viola

Violoncello

(See Barlines, Scores)

# Breath mark

The breath mark ( **,** ) has two similar uses:

- **an actual breath indication** for instruments (including voice) requiring the breath to sound.

- **a small pause or break** (as if taking a breath) for instruments *not* requiring breath to sound.

**A breath mark may or may not interrupt the tempo.** If it does interrupt the tempo, the break or pause is shorter than that of a caesura or fermata.

## PLACEMENT

The breath mark is indicated just above the staff, at the point **where a breath or break is desired.**

If the breath mark occurs between two notes, the placement is toward the **end of the space for the full value** of the note.

If the breath mark occurs at the end of a measure, the placement is just **before the barline.**

# *Caesura*

The caesura ( // ) is a small pause or break in the tempo (implying a break in sound).

> The pause of the caesura is **slightly longer than a breath mark,** but shorter than a fermata.

## PLACEMENT

> The caesura is placed on the **fourth line from the bottom** of the staff (extending to the first leger line), at the point **where a break is desired.**

> The caesura is placed toward the **end of the full value** of the note.

If space is tight, the caesura **can be centered** between two notes.

If the caesura occurs at the end of a measure, the placement is just **before the barline.**

If a longer pause is desired, **a fermata may be placed above** the caesura.

# Chord frames & symbols

Chord frames are diagrams that contain all the information necessary to play a particular chord on a fretted instrument.

*The photograph below shows the finger numbers corresponding to the fingerings used for guitar.*

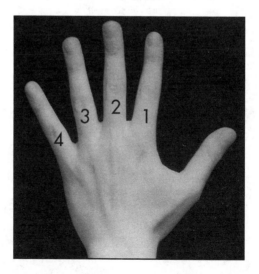

The number of strings and tunings vary between string instruments. The **chord frame is modified** (number of strings, tunings) according to the differences between each instrument.

The following examples explain the various **chord frame elements** for guitar.

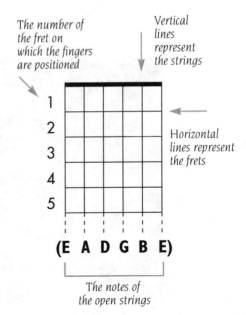

*The number of the fret on which the fingers are positioned*

*Vertical lines represent the strings*

*Horizontal lines represent the frets*

**(E  A  D  G  B  E)**

*The notes of the open strings*

The **fingerings, note names** and **position** of the chord on the neck are all provided on the chord frame.

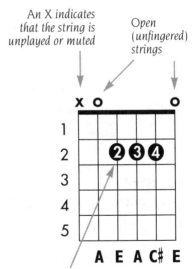

An X indicates that the string is unplayed or muted

Open (unfingered) strings

Circles indicate the fret and string on which the finger is placed— the number indicates which finger is used

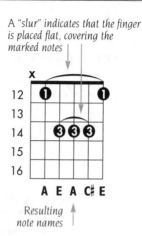

A "slur" indicates that the finger is placed flat, covering the marked notes

Resulting note names

## CHORD SYMBOLS

The **chord symbol** is always placed above the frame to identify the chord.

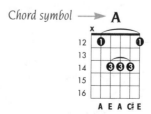

Chord symbol → **A**

Careful attention must be given to the
**consistent identification** of chords, in the
**least ambiguous way** possible.

**Chord symbols often appear without a
frame.** Whether or not there is a frame,
space must be allowed so that the symbol
is **aligned with the proper beat.**

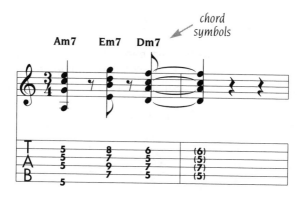

(See *Tablature*)

*A complete listing of guitar chords, along with
chord theory, is provided in* Alfred's Guitar
Chord Encyclopedia (Item #4432).
*It also includes a listing of chord symbols and
a listing of ambiguously named symbols.*

# Circle of fifths
# Clef signs

See *Key signatures*

The following are commonly used clefs.

*Middle C is shown for comparison in all examples except neutral clefs.*

## TREBLE AND BASS CLEFS

**Treble and bass clefs** are most frequently used. Keyboard, harp and organ music is written using only these clefs.

*treble clef*

*middle C*

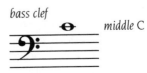

*bass clef*

*middle C*

The **octave treble clef** is sometimes used for tenor vocal parts, to indicate that the part is one octave lower than written.

The **double treble clef** serves the same function as the octave treble clef but is much less frequently seen.

*octave treble clef*      *double treble clef*

middle C

The regular **treble clef** is also commonly used for tenor vocal parts; the octave is assumed.

*treble clef for tenor voice*

middle C

## C CLEFS

**Alto clef** is commonly used for viola, to avoid excessive leger lines. (Viola also uses treble clef.)

*alto clef*

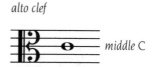

*middle* C

**Tenor clef** is primarily used for bassoon, cello and trombone when playing in higher registers.

*tenor clef*

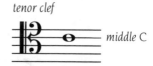

*middle* C

The following C clefs are **obsolete:**

*soprano clef*                      *mezzo-soprano clef*

*baritone clef*

## NEUTRAL CLEFS

**Neutral clefs** are used by percussion instruments of indefinite pitch. The following is most commonly used.

Neutral clef for single-line percussion:

## POSITIONING

Clefs are **slightly indented on the staff,** to the right of a systemic barline or the open single staff. Be sure to leave the *single* **staff open—do not put a barline before the clef!**

*indent on single staff—no left barline*

*indent on staff with systemic barline*

The clef is always **placed before the key signature and time signature.**

> Notice the distance from the end of the staff to the clef, from the clef to the key signature, and from the key signature to the time signature.

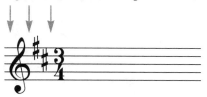

## CLEF CHANGES

When the clef changes **within a staff,** a cue-size clef is used (usually 75% of the original clef size).  Courtesy clefs are also cue size.

**If a clef change affects a complete measure,** it is always placed before the barline.

> Only a *systemic* barline can precede a clef sign.                    (See *Systems*)

**If a clef change is within a measure,** the clef is placed directly before the first note involved.

If a clef change **begins after a rest and is on a beat,** the clef is placed directly before the first note affected.

If a clef change **begins after a rest but is not on a beat,** the clef precedes the rest.

If a clef change **occurs at the beginning of a staff,** a courtesy clef is placed before the barline at the end of the previous staff, followed by the new clef at full size in the new staff.

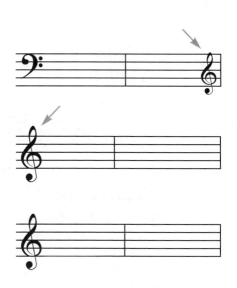

The rules for clef changes are not affected by the **addition of a key change and/or time signature change.** The clef sign precedes the barline; the key signature and time signature follow the barline.

*open staff*

Notice that the **order** of courtesy clef, key signature and time signature is the same as the order at the beginning of a piece.

The **courtesy clef** is cue size; the key signature and time signature are normal size.

Also notice the **open staff** after the *courtesy* key signature and time signature.

# Coda sign    See D.C. *al Coda,* D.S. *al Coda*

# Courtesy accidentals    See Accidentals

# *Credits*

Credits may consist of the **composer**, **lyricist** and **arranger,** or a word such as *traditional, anonymous, folk song,* etc.

1. The **composer** credit is placed flush right with the page margin.  It is not horizontally aligned with the tempo marking.

2. The **arranger** credit is placed below the composer credit (also not horizontally aligned with the tempo marking).

3. The **lyric** credit is placed flush left with the page margin, horizontally aligned with the composer credit.

*The typeface for all three credits is usually Roman.*

**For a less formal style,** such as pop piano/vocal music, the lyric credit would go under the composer credit, with the arranger under that. **All credits would be flush right** with the page margin.

Some examples:

Words and Music by...................

Words and Music by
................................

Music by...................
Words by...................
Arranged by...................

The word "arranged" may be abbreviated (Arr.).

# Cue notes

Cue notes may be given as guidance only, **to assist a performer's entrance** after numerous measures of rest.

Cue notes may also be given for **possible performance** if the cue instrument is weak or missing.   (See *Alternating instruments*)

The size of cue notes is somewhat **smaller than normal note size,** but still large enough to be legible (65–75% of normal note size).

**All musical elements associated** with the cue notes will also be at **cue size.**

There are **two ways to notate** cue passages.

With **reverse stem direction** and added rests:

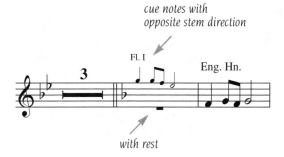

*cue notes with opposite stem direction*

*with rest*

With **normal stem direction** and no added rests:

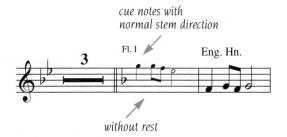

*cue notes with normal stem direction*

*without rest*

**Piano accompaniment parts** may include a cue-size solo part above the grand staff.

Not all notes that are cue *size* are used as a cue.

**Ossia passages** and **grace notes** are typically notated at cue size.    (See Ossia, Grace notes)

*grace note*

# D.C. *al* Coda (*da capo al coda*)

Means go back to the beginning, play to the "to coda" sign (⊕), then jump to the coda to finish the piece.

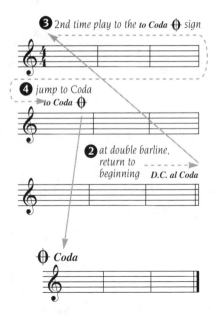

❶ *play from beginning to* **D.C. al Coda**

❸ 2nd time play to the *to Coda* ⊕ *sign*

❹ jump to Coda
→ *to Coda* ⊕

❷ *at double barline,*
*return to*
*beginning*  **D.C. al Coda**

⊕ *Coda*

**Align the edge** of the "to coda" sign
**flush right** with the barline.

The words *to Coda* are often omitted
from the "to coda" sign.

Place a **double barline** (thin/thin) at the
*D.C. al Coda.*   (*D.C. al Coda* can also be
written *D.C. al Coda* ⊕)

*add double barline*

**Separate** the coda from the staff above
(optional) and **indent**.

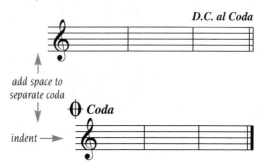

**Align** the coda sign with the beginning of
the staff. It should be somewhat **larger**
than the "to coda" sign.

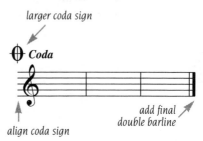

The coda will end with a **final double
barline** (thin/thick).

It is sometimes necessary to begin the coda
on the same staff as the ***D.C. al Coda.***  If so,
**break the staff** and **add a clef and key
signature.**  (Do not add a time signature
unless it changes at the coda.)

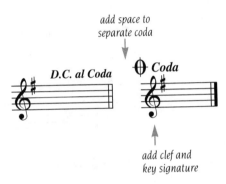

*add space to
separate coda*

*D.C. al Coda*     *Coda*

*add clef and
key signature*

# D.C. *al Fine* (da capo al fine)

Means go back to the beginning and play
to the *Fine.*

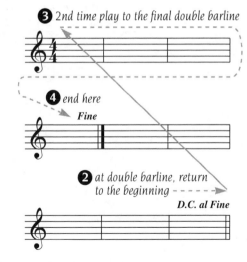

**①** *play from beginning to* **D.C. al Fine**

**③** *2nd time play to the final double barline*

**④** *end here*

*Fine*

**②** *at double barline, return
to the beginning*

**D.C. al Fine**

Place a **double barline** (thin/thin) at the *D.C. al Fine*.

*add double barline*

A **final double barline** (thin/thick) is added at the *Fine*.

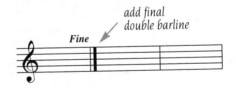

*add final double barline*

# D.S. al Coda (dal segno al coda)

Means go back to the sign (𝄋), play to the "to coda" sign (⨁), then jump to the coda to finish the piece.

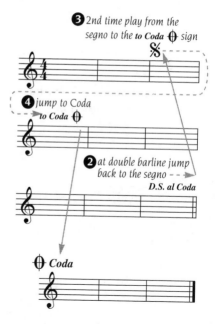

**❶** play from beginning to **D.S. al Coda**

**❸** 2nd time play from the segno to the **to Coda** ⨁ sign

**❹** jump to Coda
to Coda ⨁

**❷** at double barline jump back to the segno
**D.S. al Coda**

⨁ **Coda**

The segno 𝄋 should be **aligned flush left** with the barline.

**Align the edge** of the "to coda" sign **flush right** with the barline.

The words *to Coda* are often omitted from the "to Coda" sign.

Place a **double barline** (thin/thin) at the *D.S. al Coda*. (*D.S. al Coda* can also be written *D.S.* 𝄋 *al Coda* ⊕.)

*D.S. al Coda*

*add double barline*

**Separate** the coda from the staff above (optional) and **indent**.

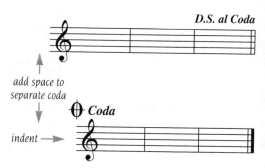

**Align** the coda sign with the beginning of the staff. It should be somewhat **larger** than the "to coda" sign.

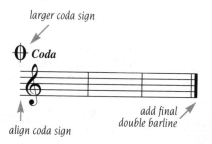

The coda will end with a **final double barline** (thin/thick).

# D.S. *al* Fine **(dal segno al fine)**

Means go back to the sign and
play to the *Fine*.

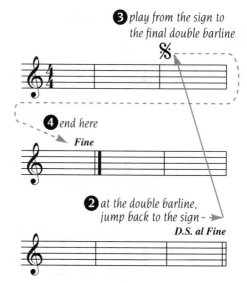

❶ *play from beginning to* **D.S. al Fine**

❸ *play from the sign to
the final double barline*

❹ *end here*

*Fine*

❷ *at the double barline,
jump back to the sign*

**D.S. al Fine**

The segno 𝄋 should be **aligned flush left** with the barline.

Add a **double barline** (thin/thin) at the *D.S. al Fine.*

*add double barline*

A **final double barline** (thin/thick) is added at the *Fine.*

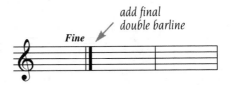

# Divisi

> **Divisi** is used for instruments (such as strings) that can produce **more than one note at a time,** indicating that the notes should be divided among the *group* of instruments (i.e., instead of multiple stops).                    (See *Sharing a staff*)

# Divisi dots                    See *Tremolo*

# Dotted rhythms          See *Augmentation dot*

# Dynamics

> Dynamics indicate the varying degree of volume or intensity of a note, phrase or section of music.

> > The following lists the most common dynamics from the softest to the loudest:

*softest* ⟶ *loudest*

$$\textit{ppp} \quad \textit{pp} \quad \textit{p} \quad \textit{mp} \quad \textit{mf} \quad \textit{f} \quad \textit{ff} \quad \textit{fff}$$

> > Dynamics **softer than *ppp* or louder than *fff* are impractical,** although theoretically any dynamic is possible.

## COMBINED DYNAMICS

Dynamics such as *mf*, *f*, *sf* can be combined with *p* or *pp*. The resulting dynamics function as a somewhat broader form of articulation.

$$fp \qquad sfp \qquad sfpp$$

*fp* would mean to play loudly, then immediately play softly.

(See Articulations)

## CRESCENDO & DIMINUENDO

The **crescendo sign** is wedge-shaped and **opens toward the right.**

The **diminuendo sign** is wedge-shaped and **opens toward the left.** (The words *diminuendo* and *decrescendo* are interchangeable, but *diminuendo* is preferred.)

A crescendo or diminuendo sign is used when a **gradual increase or decrease** is wanted from one dynamic to another.

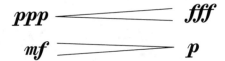

**Musical elements should not be placed within** the opening of the signs.

The word *crescendo* or *diminuendo* (*decrescendo*) may be written or abbreviated *cresc., dim. (decresc.).*

The **effect is identical** whether using the sign, word or abbreviation.

If space doesn't allow the use of the sign, or the passage is a long one, it is best to use the word.

A **dashed line** may be used if it helps clarify the length of the passage.

The word is sometimes **hyphenated** to extend throughout a section of music.

## GENERAL PLACEMENT

Place the dynamic sign *slightly* before the notehead whenever possible.

## For single-staff instruments

Dynamics are placed **below the staff.**

*dynamics below for instruments*

**When two parts share a staff** and the dynamics vary between parts, the dynamics will be placed above and below the staff.

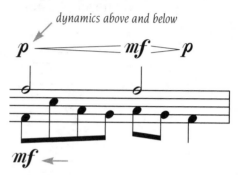

*dynamics above and below*

## For vocal music

Dynamics are placed **above the staff** to avoid conflicting with the lyric.

*dynamics above for vocal*

I    will   nev - er   cease   to   see

## For the grand staff

Dynamics are placed **between the two staves.**

**If two different dynamics** are needed for each staff, the dynamics may be placed above for the top staff and below for the bottom, or in positions that clarify the situation best.

**Horizontal placement** is preferred for crescendo and diminuendo signs, although an angled placement is acceptable if necessary.

The signs may also be **placed outside the staff** if space is tight within the grand staff.

If a dynamic mark must be placed on a barline, the barline should be **broken.**

For crescendo and diminuendo signs, the **barline is left intact.**

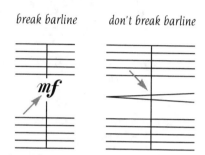

*break barline*          *don't break barline*

## Dynamics with crescendo/diminuendo signs

The intensity of the increase/decrease in volume is **relative to the dynamic level** of the section of music.

*If a dynamic is not indicated at the end of a crescendo sign, and the music is consistently gentle, the increase in volume would probably be subtle.*

The **level at the beginning of the sign** is the same as **the dynamic last indicated** in the music.

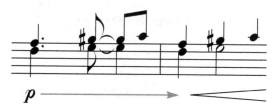

It is advised to **carefully begin and end the sign** so that it makes sense.

While the example below would make perfect sense in a clarinet part, it would make no sense in a piano part.

# Endings

See *Repeat signs*

# Fermata

A hold or pause sign ( ⌢ ). It is used with any rhythmic value—single notes, intervals, chords or rests.

## PLACEMENT

**Preferred placement is above**, regardless of stem direction, except when parts share a staff.

The fermata is **centered on the notehead** (or rest), whether it is on the notehead side or the stem side.

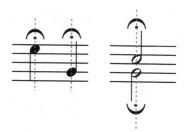

**One fermata applies to all** notes of an interval or chord.

**Place outside the staff** if at all possible.

**Place outside articulations and slurs.**

**Place the fermata on the exact beat** that is to be held, so that there can be no confusion.  In the first example below, it might be wondered whether the fermata over the whole notes would apply to the eighth rest in the lower voice.

*Confusing:*

*Same example, more clearly written:*

## TIME VALUE

A fermata over a note or chord not only indicates that the tempo is interrupted but that the note or chord is **sustained.**

The length of a fermata is **determined by the performer** and is relative to the musical situation.

*In a fast tempo, placed on a sixteenth note, the fermata would be a shorter value than if placed on a whole note, in a slow tempo.*

## USING WITH RESTS

In the following example, the fermata **prolongs silence rather than sound.**

## ABOVE A CAESURA

The following example is similar to the last one.  The caesura indicates a small break in the sound; the addition of a *fermata* **lengthens the break.**

Occasionally a fermata is seen over a final double barline before another movement. However, since a barline has no time value, **avoid using a fermata over a single barline.**

## ACCOMPANYING TERMS

**Lunga** (*long*) or **poco** (*little* or *short*) may be used with a *fermata* for a more specific intent.

These should be **centered above** the *fermata*.

# Fingerings (for keyboard)

## GENERAL PLACEMENT

Fingerings for the **right hand** should be placed **above** the staff, away from all musical elements.

Fingerings for the **left hand** should be placed **below** the staff, away from all musical elements.

*right hand above*

*left hand below*

Fingerings are **centered** above or below the notehead, when possible.

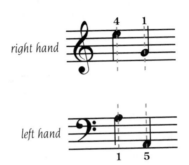

*right hand*

*left hand*

A finger number is preferably placed **outside a beam.**

## CHORDS

Fingerings are **stacked above or below** a chord; all notes should have a fingering.

If a chord includes **notes that are tied** and a fingering is indicated for a note that is *not tied*, only that fingering is necessary.

## ALTERNATING FINGERINGS

If a fingering changes on a note that is
held, a hyphen (-) or an "en-dash" (–)
**separates the two fingerings.** The first
fingering is centered on the note; the
second is to the right.

An alternate method uses a small slur
instead of the hyphen or en-dash.

## USE WITH TRIPLETS

The triplet **3** is sometimes mistaken for a fingering when the fonts are similar.

> The **fingering font should be smaller** and of a **different typeface** than the font used for triplets.

> **Avoid positioning the triplet *3* on the same side** of the staff as a fingering.

> Instead of moving the fingering, **move the triplet *3*** to the opposite side from the fingering.  The triplet *3* would normally be on the *beam* side; **if on the notehead side** it is helpful to **add a bracket.**  (See *Tuplets*)

*size and font different*

*move triplet*
*and add bracket*

# TWO HANDS ON ONE STAFF

If both hands share the same staff, the fingering for the **right hand is above,** the **left hand below.**

**RH** (right hand) or **LH** (left hand) may be added for **clarification.**

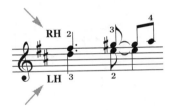

# AMOUNT OF FINGERING

Fingering should be **used sparingly** and only to establish a pattern or hand position.

## OVERLAPPING ELEMENTS

Fingerings **may overlap a slur.** The preference is to break the slur at the point of intersection, if possible.

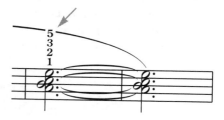

The vertical space sometimes dictates that fingerings be placed within the staff. The **staff lines should be broken** to accommodate the overlapping fingerings.

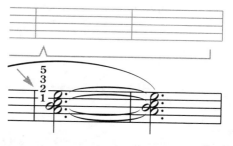

## Flat

See Accidentals, Key signatures

## Glissando sign

A glissando is indicated by a wavy or straight line placed at an angle, ascending or descending.

**Indicate the beginning and ending notes** of the glissando.

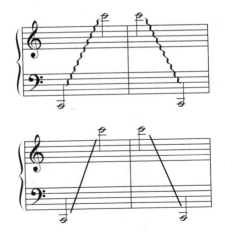

## ADD THE ABBREVIATION

It is helpful to **add the abbreviation (*gliss.*),** placing it at the same angle as the symbol.

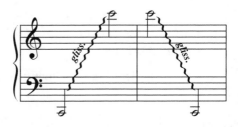

## TWO OR MORE NOTES

If the glissando affects more than one note, add a **glissando symbol for each note.** The word (*gliss.*) is used only once regardless of the number of notes.

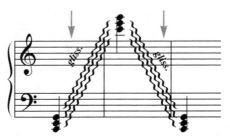

## BEGINNING AND ENDING NOTES

The **beginning and ending** of the glissando should be identified as much as possible.  This can be done in a variety of ways, depending upon the situation.

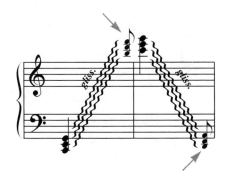

## INSTRUMENT CONSIDERATIONS

Not all instruments can play a glissando.

Careful research into the technical capabilities of each instrument is necessary.

# *Grace notes*

Grace notes are small notes **without a rhythmic value** of their own, taking their value from the previous or following beat.

Grace notes are notated at **cue size** or slightly smaller (65% of normal size works well).

### SINGLE GRACE NOTES

Single grace notes are **usually eighth notes.**

Place the **stem up** regardless of the main note's stem direction (except when two parts share a staff).

Usually a **small slur connects** the grace note to the main note; the slur usually begins below the grace note.

The slur **end does not need to be centered** on the main notehead like slurs normally do.  It may end **slightly to the left** of the notehead.          (See *Slurs*)

For single grace notes with a flag, a **small line** can intersect the flag, always **slanting upward, from left to right,** regardless of stem direction.

*(for a lower voice sharing a staff)*

## PLACEMENT ON THE STAFF

The grace note is centered in a space or placed directly on a line.

Grace-note **accidentals** are also cue size. (See *Accidentals*)

Stems for grace notes on leger lines do not have to be lengthened to meet the middle line.

## SHARING A STAFF

**When two parts share a staff,** the grace note stems follow the stem direction of the parts.

## MULTIPLE GRACE NOTES

Multiple grace notes should **never have a slanted line** through the stems or beams. The slanted line is only for single, flagged grace notes.

If a slur is used, the **slur connects** all the grace notes **to the main note.**

Two grace notes are **considered sixteenth notes** and should be beamed accordingly. Three and four can be either sixteenth or 32nd notes.

*Larger groupings, such as five and six grace notes, are usually beamed as 32nd notes.*

## DIRECTION OF GRACE-NOTE SLURS

If a grace note precedes an interval or chord, the **slur will follow the direction of resolution** (from the grace note to the appropriate main note).

## WITH LEGER LINES

If leger lines are used, the slur may be **placed above to avoid the leger lines.**

*The grace-note leger lines can be the same thickness as staff lines, but shorter.*

# Grand pause

The grand pause or general pause (G.P.) over a measure of rest indicates that the **entire orchestra is silent,** often unexpectedly.

# Grand staff

The grand staff is used to notate scores for instruments such as piano, organ, harp and marimba.

The grand staff consists of **two staves joined by a brace** and a systemic barline.

(See Brace)

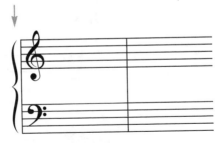

Although the "normal" clefs for the grand staff are treble above and bass below, **either staff may have either clef,** and may change clefs at any time.   (See Clef signs)

## FOR ORGAN

**Organ scores** use the grand staff connected to a staff used to notate music for the organ pedals.

Except for the systemic barline, **barlines are separated** between the manuals and pedal.

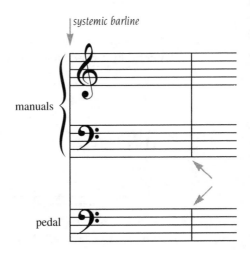

## FOR INSTRUMENT & PIANO

Scores for an instrument (including voice) and piano use a **grand staff, with the instrument staff above.**

The staff above the grand staff is sometimes **cue size,** if the instrument has its own full-size, separate part.

Except for the systemic barline, **barlines are broken** between the instrument staff and the grand staff.

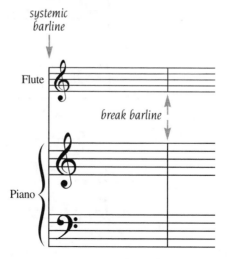

## TWO-PIANO MUSIC

Two-piano music requires two grand staves joined together with a **systemic barline**.

The measure **barlines connect staves for each grand staff only.**

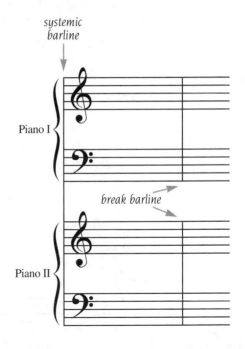

## ONE PIANO—FOUR HANDS

**Facing pages are required.**

The **Secondo** part is notated on the left-hand page; usually both staves are in **bass clef**.

The **Primo** part is notated on the right-hand page; usually both staves are in **treble clef**.

The **page layout** for primo and secondo **is preferably identical**, system-for-system; if they are not identical, the facing pages *must* begin and end with the same measures.

# *Harmonics*

## NATURAL HARMONICS

Natural harmonics are indicated by a **small circle** centered above the notehead.

The indicated note is the SOUNDING NOTE.

Such notation indicates a **natural harmonic.**

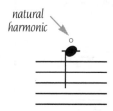

*natural harmonic*

*Careful consideration of an instrument's capabilities is necessary.  Only some instruments are capable of producing harmonics.*

Another way to notate a natural harmonic (for strings) is to use a **diamond-shaped notehead.**

The position on the staff **indicates where the finger is placed**—NOT the sounding note.

**The sounding note may be indicated** in cue size and in parentheses.

*sounding note*

*fingered note*

## ARTIFICIAL HARMONICS (STRINGS)

A diamond-shaped notehead with a standard notehead comprises an artificial harmonic. The **standard notehead indicates the placed finger**; the diamond indicates where the second finger lightly touches the node to produce the harmonic.

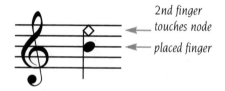

*2nd finger touches node*

*placed finger*

Often the sounding note is indicated in cue size and in parentheses.

# Key signatures

Key signatures appear **after the clef but before the time signature.**

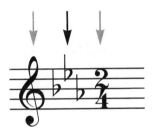

## CHANGING KEYS

The preference is to make key changes at the beginning of a staff or system, with a **courtesy key signature** at the end of the previous one.

1. A key change is traditionally preceded by a **double barline.**

2. If the key change is at the beginning of a staff or system, a **courtesy key signature** is placed at the end of the previous one.

3. The **staff is left open** after the courtesy key signature.

4. The **new key signature is indicated** on the next staff.

If a key **changes mid-staff:**

1. a double barline is added,

2. followed by the new key signature.

3. The new key signature continues on the next staff.

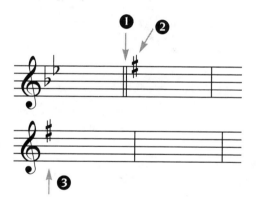

## CANCELLATIONS

**Cancellations** are no longer considered necessary, unless the new key is C major or A minor (no sharps or flats). In that case, cancel the old sharps or flats with natural signs, in the same order as the old key signature (see example on the following page).

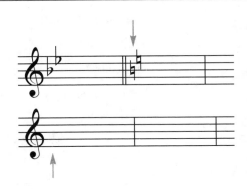

The following illustrates the positioning of the clef, key signature and time signature if all three change simultaneously.

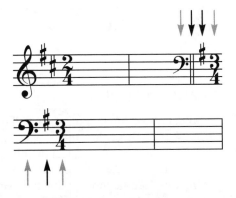

Key signatures in the **TREBLE CLEF**

Key signatures in the **BASS CLEF**

## Key signatures in the **TENOR CLEF**

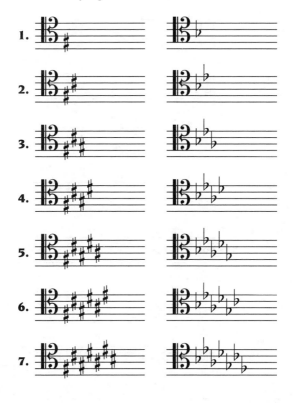

## Key signatures in the **ALTO CLEF**

## THE CIRCLE OF FIFTHS

The Circle of Fifths serves as a quick reference guide to the relationship of the keys and key signatures, and how they can be figured out in a logical manner.

The Circle of Fifths will also help to clarify which keys are enharmonic equivalents. (*Enharmonic* means notes that sound the same but are written differently.)

> **Clockwise movement** (*up a perfect 5th*) *provides all of the sharp keys by adding one sharp to the key signature progressively.*
>
> **Counter-clockwise** (*down a perfect 5th*) *provides the flat keys by adding one flat similarly.*

(See following page)

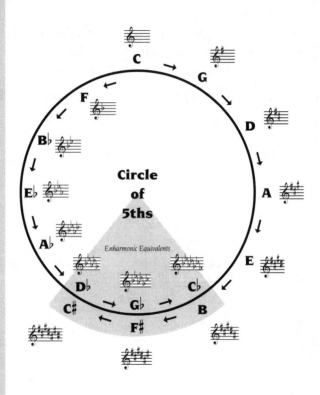

# Layout

See *Spacing*

# Leger lines

Leger lines are used to extend the range of the five-line staff.

Leger lines are the **same line weight as staff lines,** or slightly heavier.

The **vertical spacing** of leger lines must be identical to the vertical spacing between staff lines.

Leger lines **extend slightly past the notehead.** They will need to extend sufficiently enough to be seen.

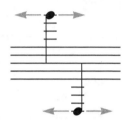

## STEM LENGTH

Stems of all notes ABOVE or BELOW the first leger line past the staff **must extend at least to the middle staff line.**

## OVERCROWDING

To avoid leger lines that touch, adjustments must be made either in the **horizontal spacing** of the music or by **shortening the leger line length.** The first is preferred, but is not always possible.

*In the first example below, the leger lines are overcrowded and appear to be touching.*

*too crowded; leger lines run together*

*Corrected by shortening the leger lines to create a slight amount of space between the lines.*

## CLEF CONSIDERATIONS

**Choose the appropriate clef** for the situation. The viola, for instance, may be written in alto clef to avoid excessive leger lines. (See Clefs)

*The following examples illustrate the same musical example in three different clefs.*

The following examples for the piano illustrate the
same music with three different clef treatments.

# Lyric

Beaming of notes associated with a lyric now follows standard notational practice.

> Traditional practice, now obsolete, was to use flags for eighth notes, sixteenth notes, etc. Beams were used only for melismas.

However, in several other ways the lyric makes the notation of a vocal part different from that of other parts.

## PLACEMENT OF STAFF INDICATIONS

> Dynamics and tempo indications go **above the staff** to avoid conflicting with the lyric.

## USE OF SLURS

Slurs are **seldom used in a vocal part for anything other than a *melisma*** (a term used here simply to mean a syllable or word that is sung to more than one note).

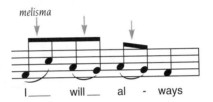

## ALIGNMENT OF LYRIC FOR MELISMA

Another help in reading a melisma is the proper **alignment of the lyric.** The word or syllable, instead of being centered under the note, should be aligned **flush left with the left edge of the notehead** (see above).

## EXTENDER LINES

In addition to the slur, **extender lines at the baseline of the lyric** help to **show the length of a melisma.** However, extender lines are only used for **one-syllable words, or for the last syllable of a word.** A hyphen is used in the middle of a word.

The **thickness of extender lines** should be less than that of the staff lines.

The **end of the extender line** should be **aligned flush right** with the last note of the melisma. *The most common mistake in the use of lyric extender lines is to extend the line for the full value of the note.*

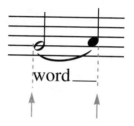

word ____

**When an extender line is called for, there should always be one,** even if the words are crowded and it has to be very short. (In this case, the line can extend slightly past the note.)

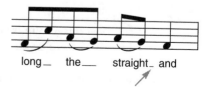

long___    the___    straight___ and

**When an extender line wraps** to the next staff, begin the line at the end of the key signature.

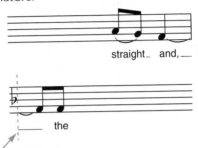

Notice the comma in the previous example.  Any **punctuation always precedes an extender line.**

TIES

**Ties are treated exactly like melismas,** including the use of extender lines and alignment of lyric.

## WORD PLACEMENT (NORMAL)

Words or syllables for notes other than melismas or tied notes are **centered to the notehead.** If the lack of space does not allow a word or syllable to be exactly centered, at least some part of the word or syllable should be under the note.

## HYPHENATED WORDS

**Center the _hyphen_** (not a dash or extender line) between syllables.

If the melisma (or tie) is extremely long, **more than one hyphen** may be used.

If the hyphenated word **wraps to the next line, another hyphen _may_ be used** at the beginning of the line.

Hyphenate words **according to the dictionary.** Do not hyphenate according to how the word *sounds* like it should divide. If there is any question at all, check the dictionary.

## PUNCTUATION

Use **normal punctuation and capitalization.** (Sometimes capitalization is done as if the words were poetry, with each "line" capped, but this is becoming less common.) A *common mistake is to use little or no punctuation.*

## MULTIPLE VERSES & REPEATS
### Broken slurs

A **broken slur** is used when one verse has a melisma, especially if it is not the first verse.

**Treat the lyric for each verse separately.** Notice in the above example that the melisma is aligned *as a melisma*, while the previous verse is aligned normally.

## Omission lines

An omission line is sometimes used to clarify that there is **no word or syllable sung.**

| Now | I | see you here | with |
| When | _ | I was quite | young, |

In many cases, however, there is a better way to treat the situation. In the previous example, the omission line could be mistaken for an extender line, so it would be better without it, letting the cue-size rest serve the same purpose.

## Cue-size notes, rests

Use cue-size notes and rests **when a rhythm is different from the first verse** (see previous example). Stems and beams should also be cue size.

If there are **more than two verses** with different rhythms, the notation can become quite complicated.  It may be better to write out the music.

## Numbering

### Multiple verses are numbered.

> $\longrightarrow$  1. Verse, verse, verse
> $\longrightarrow$  2. Verse, verse, verse
> $\longrightarrow$  3. Verse, verse, verse

There are no set rules for treatment of pick-ups, repeats, first and second endings, etc.  Be clear and consistent.

## Using a brace

When multiple lines converge into one line, such as a *chorus* or *refrain*, a **brace** is used.

$\longrightarrow$  1. Verse, verse, verse
$\longrightarrow$  2. Verse, verse, verse $\Big\}$ chorus or refrain $\longrightarrow$
$\longrightarrow$  3. Verse, verse, verse

# Meter

The understanding of meter is essential to the placement of ties, rests, syncopated rhythms and proper beaming.

**Time signatures** identify the meter.

There are two overall classifications of meter: **perfect** and **imperfect** (odd) meter.

## PERFECT METER

In perfect meter the measure can be divided into **equal halves or thirds**.

There are two classifications of perfect meter: **simple meter** and **compound meter.**

In **simple** meters each **BEAT** can be subdivided by 2.

In **compound** meters each **PULSE** can be subdivided by 3.

*Metric subdivisions should not be confused with tuplets.*

## SIMPLE METER

The classification of **duple, triple** or **quadruple** reflects the number of **BEATS** in the measure.

### Simple duple meter

Simple duple time signatures have a 2 as the upper number of the time signature.

$$\frac{2}{2} \qquad \frac{2}{4} \qquad \frac{2}{8}$$

Each measure contains **2 BEATS.**

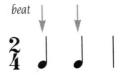

Each BEAT can be **subdivided by 2**.

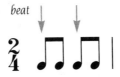

Only **rests of equal value to the beat** or less may be used (except in a complete **measure of rest,** which is indicated by a whole rest).

**Rests** of equal value to the beat are used ONLY on the beat.

*The following are all acceptable examples*
*in simple duple meter.*

*quarter note is acceptable, but not a quarter rest*

## Simple triple meter

Simple triple time signatures have a 3 as
the upper number of the time signature.

$$\frac{3}{2} \quad \frac{3}{4} \quad \frac{3}{8}$$

Each measure contains **3 BEATS**.

Each beat can be **subdivided by 2.**

Only **rests of equal value to the beat** or less may be used (except in a complete **measure of rest,** which is indicated by a whole rest).

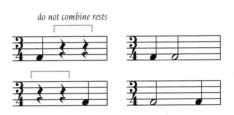

**Beaming should reflect the simple triple meter,** NOT compound duple meter.

## Simple quadruple meter

Simple quadruple time signatures have a
4 as the upper number of the time
signature.

$$\frac{4}{2} \qquad \frac{4}{4} \qquad \frac{4}{8}$$

Each measure contains **4 BEATS.**

Each beat can be **subdivided by 2.**

To successfully notate *simple quadruple*
meter, it is best to consider the meter as
a combination of **2 units of duple meter.**

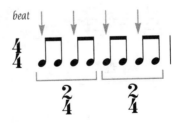

In *simple quadruple meter, these* **2 units**
*must always be clearly distinguished. The*
*only exception to this would be a very simple*
*syncopation (such as ♩♩ ♩).*

The following examples illustrate the **subdivision of the 2 units.** The notation of each unit, separately, is identical to that of simple duple meter.

**Whole rests** are used to indicate a complete measure of rest.

**Rests twice the value of the beat** are used ONLY on beats 1 & 3 (the first beat of each half of the measure).

**Rests of equal value to the beat** can ONLY appear on the beat.

**Rests less than the value of the beat** are used freely as long as the two units are apparent.

*do not combine rests*

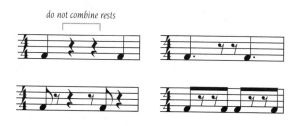

## COMPOUND METER

The classification of **duple, triple** or **quadruple** reflects the number of **PULSES** in the measure.

### Compound duple meter

Compound duple time signatures have a 6 as the upper number of the time signature.

$$\begin{matrix} \mathbf{6} \\ \mathbf{4} \end{matrix} \quad \begin{matrix} \mathbf{6} \\ \mathbf{8} \end{matrix}$$

Each measure contains **2 PULSES.**

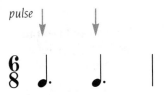

Each PULSE can be **divided into 3 BEATS.**

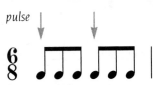

Only **rests of equal value to the pulse** or less may be used (except in a complete **measure of rest** which is indicated by a whole rest).

**Rests** of equal value to the pulse can ONLY appear on the pulse.

**Rests of $2/3$ the value of a pulse** may be used ONLY on the pulse.

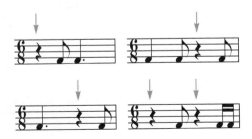

Rests of equal value to the beat, **not appearing on the pulse,** CANNOT be combined.

**Beaming should reflect the compound duple meter,** NOT simple triple meter.

## Compound triple meter

Compound triple time signatures have a 9 as the upper number of the time signature. An example is $\frac{9}{8}$.

Each measure contains **3 PULSES.**

Each PULSE can be **divided into 3 BEATS.**

Rules governing **rests and beaming** are identical to compound duple meter.

## Compound quadruple meter

Compound quadruple time signatures have a 12 as the upper number of the time signature. An example is $\frac{12}{8}$.

Each measure contains **4 PULSES.**

Each PULSE can be **divided into 3 BEATS.**

To successfully notate *compound quadruple* meter it is best to consider the meter as a combination of **2 units of compound duple meter.**

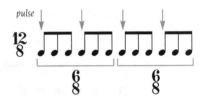

Rules governing **rests and beaming** are identical to compound duple meter.

# IMPERFECT METER (ODD METER)

In imperfect meter (odd meter) the measure **CANNOT be divided into equal halves or thirds.**

Imperfect meter can be considered as any combination of **duple or quadruple meter** AND **triple meter.**

$\frac{7}{8}$ time can be considered a combination of $\frac{2}{4} + \frac{3}{8}$ or $\frac{3}{8} + \frac{2}{4}$.

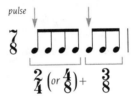

*Notice that 7 is not divisible by 2 or 3.*

# MODERN APPROACHES TO METER

A **broken barline** is sometimes added to clarify imperfect meters.

A **composite meter** is another option to clarify the subdivision of imperfect meters.

*composite meter*

When two or more measures alternate meters in a manner that repeats predictably, a time signature reflecting the **alternating meter** may be used.

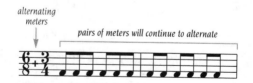

*alternating meters*

*pairs of meters will continue to alternate*

# Metronome marks
See *Tempo marks*

# Natural sign
See *Accidentals*

# Notes

Traditionally there are five main shapes representing noteheads:

| Pitched | Non-pitched |
|---|---|
| **O** *whole note* | **◇** *whole note, half note* |
| **𝑂** *half note* | |
| **●** *quarter, eighth, sixteenth, 32nd, etc.* | **X** *quarter, eighth, sixteenth, 32nd, etc.* |

## PLACEMENT ON THE STAFF

On a **five-line staff,** notes are either in a space or on a line.

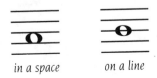

*in a space*        *on a line*

On a **single-line staff,** the notehead usually intersects the line, with the stem always up.

When two instruments share a staff, one part sits on the line; the other hangs from the line.

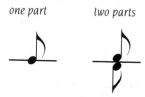

*one part*          *two parts*

## STEMS AND NOTEHEADS

**Double whole notes** (or *breves*) and **whole notes** are without stems.

‖O‖          O

*double*      *whole*
*whole*        *note*
*note*

**Half notes** and **quarter notes** are always stemmed.

*half
note*   *quarter
note*

Single **eighth, sixteenth, 32nd and 64th notes** are always stemmed and with a flag(s).

*8th
note*   *16th
note*   *32nd
note*   *64th
note*

Two or more eighth, sixteenth, 32nd and 64th notes are usually **beamed into groups.**

*8th*   *16th*   *32nd*   *64th*

An **X** notehead is used primarily in **non-pitched percussion** music. It is also seen in vocal music to indicate approximate-pitched singing (*Sprechstimme*), rhythmically spoken parts, clapping, etc.

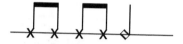

The diamond-shaped notehead serves as a half note (with stem) or whole note (without stem).

When used as a **harmonic,** the diamond-shaped **notehead is always open,** whatever the rhythmic value.

*In some software programs the characters for the diamond-shaped notehead and the harmonic are slightly different.*

# Octave signs

The use of octave signs is primarily to **avoid multiple leger lines.** While frequently used in piano music, octave signs are only selectively used in instrumental music.

*8va* or *all'ottava* means "at the octave."

> *8va* (or *8* if Italian is not used) is indicated above a **treble clef staff only.** Do not use above any other clef.
>
> Usually accompanied by an extender line— **a broken line with a downstroke** at the end.
>
> The alignment of the *8va* is centered above the notehead.
>
> The end of the *8va* bracket **extends slightly past the last note** affected.

center to
notehead

end hook down

*8va bassa* or *ottava bassa* means "at the octave below."

*8va (or 8) below the staff, especially in keyboard music, is always understood to mean **8va bassa**.*

*8va bassa* is indicated below a **bass clef staff only.**  Do not use for treble, alto or tenor clefs.

Usually accompanied by an extender line— **a broken line with an upstroke** at the end.

The beginning of the *8va bassa* is placed below the notehead.

The end of the *8va bassa* line **extends slightly past the last note** affected.

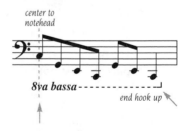

The abbreviation *8vb* is *only* a copyist's shorthand and **should not be used in engraved music.**

## PLACEMENT CONSIDERATIONS

The **8va** or **8va bassa** with its extender line should be **clearly placed,** to avoid conflict with as many musical elements as possible and yet be as close to the notes affected as possible.

*In the example below, the 8va is placed entirely above the slur.*

*In this example, the 8va intersects the slur due to a possible limitation of space.*

## WITH ACCIDENTALS

**Accidentals must be repeated** for the notes included within *8va* or *8va bassa* octave alterations.

## WRAPPING FROM STAFF TO STAFF

The *8va* or *8va bassa* **breaks at the end of the first staff,** aligned with the right barline.

The extender line **begins again just past the clef** or key signature.

A **courtesy** *8va* or *8va bassa* may also be indicated at the beginning of the second staff when wrapping from staff to staff.

## LOCO

Although the ending of the extender line should suffice, the word *loco* (meaning "at place") may be added as a reminder that the *8va* or *8va bassa* no longer applies.

## ON AN ENDING NOTE

The *8va* or *8va bassa* **is centered to the notehead** and, since it is the last note of the piece, it may or may not be accompanied with a downstroke (or upstroke).

If a single note is altered but is **not the last note** of the piece, an **upstroke (or downstroke)** *must* be added.

## SPECIAL SITUATIONS

The following examples are incorrectly notated.  The *8va* or *8va bassa* is **never placed between the two staves** of a grand staff.

These two incorrect examples would need to be rewritten—perhaps in one of the following ways:

Rewritten either:

or:

## WITH RESTS

If the *8va* or *8va bassa* is interrupted with short rests, the **extender line may continue over** them.

If the rests are of a **larger value, the line should be broken** and reintroduced.

When **rests precede** the *8va* or *8va bassa,* begin on the first note after the rests.

When **rests follow** the *8va* or *8va bassa,* the octave alteration ends with the last note in the grouping—the rests should not be included in the grouping.

## CUE SIZE

For any passage at **cue size** the *8va* will likewise be at cue size.

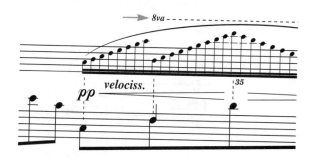

# 15MA

**15ma** or *quindicesima* means "at the fifteenth" (two octaves).  The situations to use **15ma bassa** are very rare.

All rules for *8va* apply to *15ma*.

# COLL' 8VA

*Coll' 8va* (or *coll' 8*) is an abbreviation for *coll' ottava* meaning **"with the octave."**  It is a shorthand system of writing octaves, **discouraged in traditional engraving.**

The function of *coll' 8va* differs from *8va* in that the written notes are **doubled at the octave.**

For the extender line, a longer dash length or a solid line is recommended, to make the ***coll' 8va*** distinguishable from ***8va***.

The ***coll' 8va*** doubles at the **octave above** when notated in the **treble clef**.

*is played:*

The ***coll' 8va*** doubles at the **octave below** when notated in the **bass clef**.

*is played:*

## INSTRUMENT CONSIDERATIONS

### ORCHESTRA / BAND SCORES

Often a score will have **limited space,** causing leger lines to become too crowded and illegible. Octave signs help to **eliminate vertical overcrowding.**

### WOODWINDS

Wind players prefer to read leger lines.

### STRINGS

Octave signs should be used very sparingly for viola and cello. Violins are accustomed to reading either leger lines or *8va* (but not *15ma*).

### KEYBOARD INSTRUMENTS

**Celesta** uses *8va* but not *8va bassa* (the range does not extend low enough).

**Harpsichord** rarely uses *8va* or *8va bassa.* Leger lines are more commonly used.

**Piano** uses *8va* and *15ma* in the treble clef and *8va bassa* in the bass clef.

**Organ** uses *8va* but not *8va bassa* (the range does not extend low enough).

# Ornaments

Ornaments are primarily used in Baroque, Classical or Romantic period music. The interpretation of an ornament **varies according to the musical period** or composer. It is advised to consult detailed references on ornament usage and interpretation.

Ornament symbols are **placed above the staff** regardless of stem direction.

**When two parts share a staff,** an ornament symbol applying to the lower part is placed below the staff.

Ornaments are usually **centered** to the notehead. **Depending upon the position** of the ornament, the realization of the ornament will vary.

*In the example below, the turn symbol is presented two ways, centered above the note and positioned after the note.*

*Notice the different realizations of the ornament.*

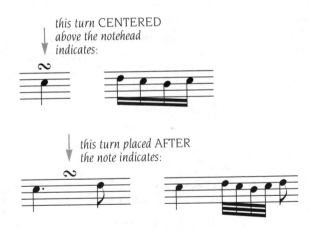

*this turn CENTERED above the notehead indicates:*

*this turn placed AFTER the note indicates:*

For placement of ornament realizations in the music see *Ossia*.

# Ossia

Ossia is an indication for an **alternate version,** which may be easier or more difficult.  It is treated the same as a realized ornament.

The ossia passage (or ornament) is **placed above** a single-line staff.  (Place above and/or below a grand staff.)  The passage is cue size (65–75%).

Only the **passage concerned is notated**— the staff begins directly before and ends directly after.  (Common practice is not to use a clef, time signature or key signature.)

**Align** all beats.

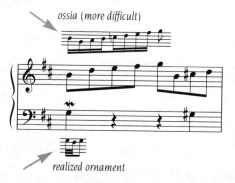

*ossia (more difficult)*

*realized ornament*

# Pedal marks

## FOR THE PIANO

There are three pedals on a grand piano: the **damper pedal** (right), the **sostenuto pedal** (center) and the **una corda pedal** (left). Some upright pianos have only two pedals—the damper and una corda.

### Damper pedal

Markings for the damper pedal (sustain pedal) are **always placed below the grand staff** and are usually placed below all other musical elements.

The most commonly used pedal marks consist of three elements: *pedal down*, *pedal change* and *pedal up*.

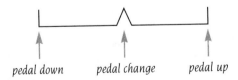

*pedal down*          *pedal change*          *pedal up*

The **pedal-down marking** begins vertically aligned with the left edge of the notehead.*

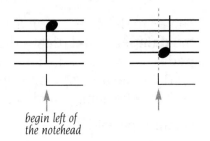

*begin left of
the notehead*

The *point* of the **pedal-change marking** is vertically aligned with the center of the notehead.

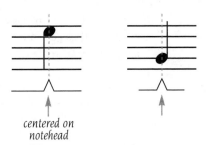

*centered on
notehead*

*Some publishers center or align flush right. In any case, a style decision should be made.

The **pedal-up marking** is vertically aligned to the left of the notehead.

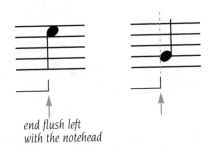

*end flush left
with the notehead*

The traditional method of pedal marking consisted of **pedal down** and **pedal up.**

*This method is somewhat obsolete.*

*pedal down*            *pedal up*

Drawbacks of this method of pedal indication include the potential for inaccuracy and a cluttered look.

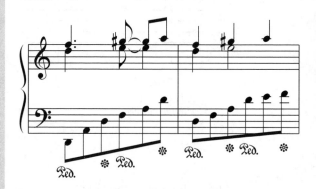

## Flutter Pedal

To notate the rapid fluctuating of the pedal, a **zigzag pattern** interrupts the usual pedal marking.

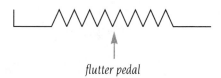

*flutter pedal*

## Wrapping from staff to staff

The pedal mark is interrupted at the end of the staff. It continues on the next staff, **beginning immediately after the key signature.**

If the pedal mark continues to the end of the piece, it is vertically aligned with the thin line of the final double barline.

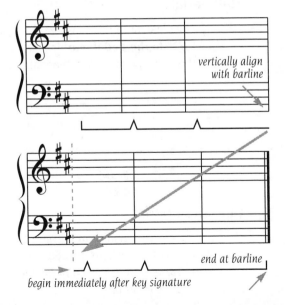

*vertically align with barline*

*end at barline*

*begin immediately after key signature*

## Simile

When the pattern **has been clearly established**, *simile* may be used instead of continuing the pedal marks.    (See *Simile*)

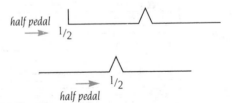

If the pattern changes, simply begin the pedal marks again.

## Half pedal

The clearest indication is to simply **add "1/2" to the pedal marking,** whether at the down pedal or at the pedal change.

## Una corda pedal

The indication **una corda** (one string) or **u.c.** is placed where the pedal is pressed; **tre corde** (three strings) or **t.c.** indicates the return to normal.

## Sostenuto pedal

This is indicated by the abbreviation *sos.*
(sometimes in combination with a bracket).

*sos.* ⌐‾‾‾‾‾‾‾⌐

## FOR THE ORGAN

Two symbols are used, one for the *heel*,
one for the *toe*.

U          ∧
*heel*          *toe*

The symbols are **NOT inverted** when
moved from one side of the staff to
the other.

The pedal marks for the right foot are
always **placed above the staff and
centered on the notehead.**

*right-foot heel*                *right-foot toe*

The pedal marks for the left foot are always **placed below the staff and centered on the notehead.**

*left-foot heel*          *left-foot toe*

Changes from *toe to heel* or *heel to toe* while sustaining a note require **a small slur** to connected the markings.

Slur placement is **above for right-foot** markings—**below for left-foot** markings.

**Foot changes** are indicated by placing right and left foot markings above and below the same note.

*change from left
to right foot*

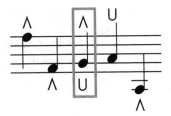

If a **foot change occurs on a tied note,** one foot is indicated on the first tied note and the other foot on the second tied note.

## HARP PEDALS

Pedal indications for harp are **settings for tuning.**

The left and right foot have **separate sets** of pedals.

Notation for the harp is closely linked to the position of each of these pedals. Therefore, **enharmonic spellings** are frequent in harp music.

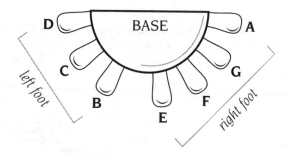

The tuning of the harp is based on the three **notch positions** of the pedals.

When a pedal is in its resting position, **center,** the string is tuned to the note's letter name (D, C, B, E, F, G & A).

When a pedal is **raised,** the note is lowered a half step (loosens the string).

When a pedal is **lowered,** the note is raised a half step (tightens the string).

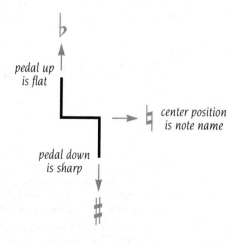

*pedal up is flat*

*center position is note name*

*pedal down is sharp*

The following three examples illustrate possible ways to indicate harp pedal settings in a score.

They may be listed **horizontally, stacked or using the Salzedo diagram.**

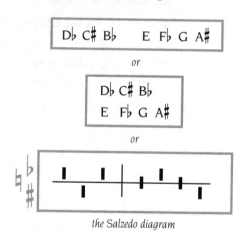

*the Salzedo diagram*

PEDALS AND THE USE OF ACCIDENTALS

The positioning of the pedals dictates which accidentals are to be used. Sometimes the choice of accidentals may not fit into a theoretical framework but is determined by the best possible pedal settings for the harpist.

# *Picking*

Picking is notated with *down-stroke* and *up-stroke* symbols. The same symbols may be used as those that are used for down-bow and up-bow.

> **Down-stroke** and **up-stroke** indications are centered to the notehead and are always placed above the staff.

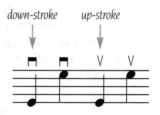

# *Repeat signs*

Indications for repeats occur on three levels: **beat repetitions, measure repetitions and section repetitions.** The first two are used almost exclusively in manuscript or in popular music.

## BEAT REPETITIONS

Angled slashes following a single beat indicate that whatever is written on the **first beat is to be repeated.** These are commonly **used in manuscript.** Do not use in engraved music.

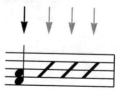

Another use of beat repeats is in **guitar or rhythm parts,** where they help pinpoint where chord changes occur. These are

used in engraved music.  Stems, beams
and ties may be used when necessary.

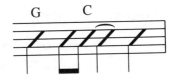

## ONE-MEASURE REPEAT

This sign (𝄎), meaning **repeat the
previous measure,** consists of a slash with
two dots and is centered in an otherwise
empty measure.  In engraved music, its use
should be limited to rhythm parts.

When several consecutive measure repeats
are used, numbering is helpful.  **Place a
small number** above the staff and **center it
on the measure repeat sign.**

The **notated measure is considered the
first measure,** with the actual numbering
beginning on the first repeated measure.

**Write out** the music **at key points** such as rehearsal numbers, page turns, etc.

## TWO-MEASURE REPEAT

When **two measures are to be repeated,** a sign consisting of *two* slashes with dots is placed **on the center bar line** of two otherwise empty measures, **with the number 2 above it.** The number is in the same typeface and size as a time signature number.

This sign should *not* be used when one measure is to be repeated twice. It should only be used for **two consecutive measures that are** *different,* and are to be repeated. In engraved music, it should only be used in rhythm parts.

If more than two measures are to be repeated, the **repeat sign** should be used.

## SECTION REPETITIONS

The **repeat sign** is used to indicate the repeat of one or more measures, or an entire section.

*The repeat sign looks like a final double barline, with two dots positioned in the spaces above and below the center line of the staff.*

The right-facing repeat sign is **placed at the beginning** of the first measure of the section to be repeated. The left-facing sign is **placed at the end** of the last measure of the same section.

Thus, the section that is to be repeated is **framed** by the inward-facing repeat signs.

*If the repeat begins **at the beginning of a piece**, the right-facing sign is not needed.

For **two adjoining repeated sections,**
repeat signs are placed, as before, framing
each section. The **adjoining repeat signs
may share the thick bar.**

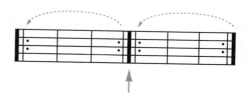

## With key changes

When a key signature change occurs at the
beginning of a repeated section, a double
bar is added and the **key signature is
placed before the first repeat sign**.

*key signature change*
*before repeat sign* ↓

## With multiple endings

A section that is repeated may have a different ending each time it is played.

The repeat sign is placed at the beginning of the section and at the last bar line of the 1st ending.

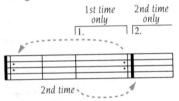

The **brackets do not intersect or touch the staff** but are placed above the staff, avoiding all musical elements. They are aligned vertically with the barlines.

1st ending brackets are **always closed.**

If the **2nd ending** is **not the end of the piece,** the bracket will be **open-ended.**

If it is the **end of the piece** (or movement), the bracket will be **closed.**

If a section is played three or more times but there are only two endings, number the brackets accordingly. This occurs often when there are lyrics.

It is possible to have *three* different endings to a section; they are treated the same as a 1st and 2nd ending.

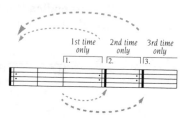

# Rests

This section deals mainly with the positioning of rests. For more on the use of rests, see Meter and Augmentation dot.

## TABLE OF RESTS

In the listing of rests below, each rest is half the value of the previous rest, starting with the double whole rest.

double whole rest    whole rest    half rest    quarter rest

eighth rest    sixteenth rest    32nd rest    64th rest

## DOUBLE WHOLE REST (BREVE)

The double whole rest is placed between the third and fourth staff lines, touching both lines.

## WHOLE REST

With the exception of $\frac{4}{2}$ and $\frac{8}{4}$, the whole rest is used to signify a **complete measure of rest** in any time signature.

It **hangs** from the fourth staff line.

Whole rests are **centered in the measure.**

When two parts share a staff, whole rests are positioned on the **fifth line for the top** part and the **first line for the bottom.**

If either part conflicts with the placement of the rest, the rest may be **positioned outside the staff.**

*upper part*

## HALF REST

The half rest is positioned to **sit on the third staff line.**

When two parts share a staff, the half rest will sit on **either the fifth line or the first line.**

If either part conflicts with this placement, the rest may be positioned **outside the staff.**

Half rests are **positioned at the beginning of beat 1 or 3**—never centered between two beats.

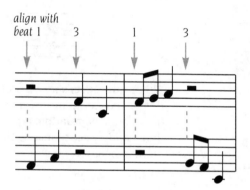

*In the above example the use of half rests instead of two quarter rests is correct. However, meter must be considered—do not automatically substitute a half rest for two quarter rests.*

(See Meter)

## QUARTER REST

The quarter rest is positioned as follows. Notice the position of the bottom hook.

**When two parts share a staff,** the quarter rest is moved **up or down** from its normal position. The **relationship** of the rest to **lines and spaces** must be the same as in normal position.

The rest may be completely outside the staff when necessary.

In some situations the above rests could be left out entirely. In other situations, if *both parts* were resting, one rest in normal position could serve for both.

## EIGHTH, SIXTEENTH & 32ND RESTS

The guidelines for positioning quarter rests in the example above also apply for eighth, sixteenth and 32nd rests.

The *hook* **of these rests is always placed in a space** (or between imaginary leger lines if placed outside the staff).

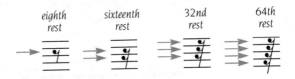

| eighth rest | sixteenth rest | 32nd rest | 64th rest |

If one of the above rests **interferes with a beam, the rest moves up or down** so that stem lengths may be more normal. Other rests in the measure remain in normal position.

## MULTIPLE-MEASURE RESTS

For a rest of more than one measure, a **horizontal line** (the thickness of a beam) is placed on the middle staff line, with a thinner vertical line at each end extending from the second to the fourth staff line.

A number the size and font of a time-signature number is placed above the staff and centered in the measure.

**Break the multiple-measure rest** for rehearsal numbers, tempo changes, etc.

## RESTS ON A SINGLE-LINE STAFF

When there is only one part on a staff, position the rests as follows:

When **two parts share a single-line staff,** place the rests above and below the line, not touching the line. Use a leger line for whole and half rests.

# *Scores*

On a complete score all parts are included on a system and are arranged in a certain order.

All information contained on the parts and score must be **identical.**

On the first page of the score the system (or first system) is **indented.** Brackets connect instrument *choirs*. (See Bracket, Systems)

The **full name of each instrument** is given to the left of the first system.

**Abbreviations** are substituted for the full instrument names on subsequent systems.

**Rehearsal numbers** (indicated at the top of the score) serve as key reference points.

They may be **letters** or **measure numbers** enclosed in a circle or square.

All **extracted parts** will have **identical rehearsal** numbers.

## SCORE ORDER

Instruments should be arranged in what is known as *score order*.

**Woodwinds**

**Brasses**

**Percussion**

**Other Instruments**

**Strings**

Each **family** of instruments is predominantly **grouped together** from highest-pitched instruments to lowest-pitched instruments, with some traditional exceptions.

*The French horns, although not the highest-pitched, are traditionally placed above the other brass instruments.*

## STRING QUARTET

Violin I
Violin II
Viola
Violoncello

## BRASS QUINTET

Trumpet I
Trumpet II
French Horn
Trombone
Tuba

## WOODWIND QUARTET

Flute
Oboe
Clarinet
Bassoon

## BRASS SEXTET

Trumpet I
Trumpet II
French Horn
Trombone
Euphonium (Baritone)
Tuba

## WOODWIND QUINTET

Flute
Oboe
Clarinet
French Horn
Bassoon

## CONCERT BAND

Flutes
Oboes
Bassoons
Clarinets
Saxophones
Cornets/Trumpets
French Horns
Trombones
Euphonium (Baritone)
Tuba
Timpani
Percussion

## JAZZ BAND (STAGE BAND)

Saxophones
Trumpets
Trombones
Guitar
String or Electric Bass
Drums
Piano

## ORCHESTRA

Flutes
Oboes
Clarinets
   [Saxophone]
Bassoons
   [Saxophone]

French Horns
Trumpets
Trombones
Tuba

Timpani
Percussion

Other instruments (harp, piano, celesta, organ, voices, chorus, solo instruments, or sometimes saxophones)

Violin I
Violin II
Viola
Violoncello
Contrabass

# Segue

See Attacca

# Sharing a staff

In band or orchestra music some parts of instrument families share the same staff. Combine parts 1 & 2 or 2 & 3; avoid combining three instruments on one staff.

## BEGINNING A PASSAGE

*If parts are divisi, no indication is necessary unless one or both instruments (such as strings) can play more than one note at a time.*     (See Divisi)

Indicate **a2** above staff if both parts play in unison.  Use only one stem per note.

If the unison continues after a page turn, repeat **a2** in parentheses.

If like instruments are sharing a staff and only one part plays, indicate which part: I. or II.

If unlike instruments are sharing the staff
and one part plays, indicate which
instrument is playing.

## STEMMING OF TWO PARTS

If two parts are playing **different pitches
but the same rhythm,** they share **one stem.**

If the parts are **alternating between unison and divisi, and share the same rhythm,** opposite stem direction makes the unisons clear.

If both parts have **different rhythms,** opposite stem direction is necessary.

(See *Accidentals, Rests*)

## FROM TWO PARTS TO UNISON

Opposite stem direction is used for clarity on **unison notes in short passages.**

Indicate *a2* above staff and use one stem for longer passages.

## FROM TWO PARTS TO ONE:

**Use rests** in shorter passages.

**Place I. or II. above the staff** and use one stem (for two *like* instruments in longer passages or after long rests).

**Mark passage with instrument name** (for two *unlike* instruments in longer passages or after long rests).

## STAFF INDICATIONS

Staff indications (dynamic, slurs, tempi) are **placed below** the staff.

*place below*

If the two parts move **independently,** a **separate set of directions** is needed for each part, above and below the staff.

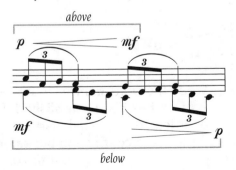

*below*

### WHEN NOT TO SHARE A STAFF

1. If the range of one part tends to cross the range of the other, the parts should have **separate staves.**
2. If the parts require **different clefs** or **clef changes** the parts should be separated.
3. If the two parts are **too rhythmically diverse,** they should be separated.

In all cases **a bracket should be used,** not a brace.

# Sharp

See Accidentals

# Simile

When the word *simile* is indicated after a **pattern has been established** (for example, of articulations, pedal marks, bowing, etc.), it means to **continue in the same manner.**

(See Articulations, Pedal marks)

# *Slurs*

Although a slur looks somewhat like a tie, the placement, positioning and use of slurs are different from ties. Slurs and ties should not be confused.

> Slurs are used to indicate phrasing or technique. Depending on the instrument, the slur will imply different techniques to be used.

## PLACEMENT OF SLURS

The **stemming** of the notes is the main factor in determining whether the slur is to be placed above or below.

> When **stems extend up,** the **slur is placed under**, on the notehead side.

When **stems extend down,** the **slur is placed over,** on the notehead side.

When **stems are in both directions,** the **slur is always placed over.**

If the notes are whole notes, *imagine* the stems!

If the **phrase is substantially long,** the slur may be placed over, regardless of stem direction.

Slurs have a **definite beginning and ending;** they should not be "hanging in space" so that the beginning and ending notes must be guessed at.

## PLACEMENT ON THE NOTEHEAD

If the slur is on the notehead side, the beginning and ending of the slur should be **centered on the notehead.** It should not touch the notehead.

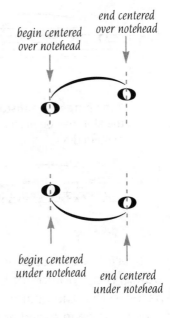

*begin centered over notehead*

*end centered over notehead*

*begin centered under notehead*

*end centered under notehead*

## BEGINNING FROM THE STEM

Place the beginning of the slur so it **starts mid-stem** (to the **right** of the stem—never begin to the left, crossing the stem).

In some cases the slur may begin **at the end of the stem.**

Begin at the end of the stem **if beaming is involved.** Never cross the beam with a slur.

## ENDING ON THE STEM

Place the end of the slur so it **slopes
towards the notehead,** away from the end
of the stem. **Center the slur** on the
notehead.

The slur may also end **at the end of the
stem** if it would make a more pleasing
shape.

End at the end of the stem **if beaming is
involved.** Never cross the beam with a slur.

## SLUR DIRECTION

If the direction of the **phrase ascends,** the slur will **slope upward.** If the direction of the **phrase descends,** the slur will **slope downward.**

When a slur **begins and ends on the same note**, the slur can remain on the same horizontal level.

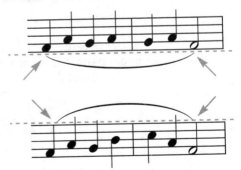

## SLURS WITH CHORDS

**Only one slur is needed** when there is only one stem per chord.

## SHARING THE SAME STAFF

For two parts, place slurs **above for the upper part, below for the lower part.**

For two *sets* of parts, place slurs **above for the upper parts, below for the lower parts.**

## WRAPPING FROM STAFF TO STAFF

**Align the end of the slur with the end of the staff.** The slur ends at an **angle** (ascending or descending) at the end of the staff.

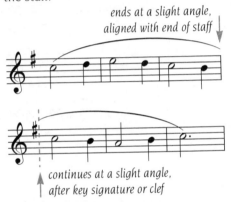

*ends at a slight angle, aligned with end of staff* ↓

*continues at a slight angle, after key signature or clef* ↑

**Continue the slur** in the lower staff immediately after the key signature (or clef), also at an **angle.** Be sure the first note is far enough to the right so that it is very clear that the slur does not begin on the note.

If the slur is over the staff it **remains over** when continuing on the next staff. If it is under, it **remains under** on the next staff.

The **direction of the slur** (ascending or descending) continues logically in the following staff.

*slur ascends to follow direction of notes*

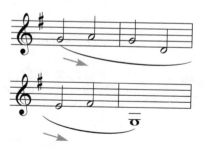

*slur descends to follow direction of notes*

# DIFFERENTIATING SLURS FROM TIES

When slurs and ties are both involved in a chord progression such as the following, **position the slur opposite to the tie** and at a noticeable **angle.**

*slur MUST be moved opposite to the tie*

*wrong*

An even better way to write the above:

If a slur **begins and ends on the same pitch** and could possibly be mistaken for a tie, position the slur on the stem side.

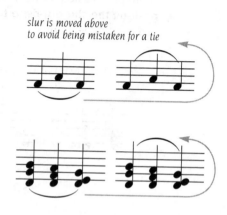

*slur is moved above to avoid being mistaken for a tie*

When a slur connects chords with **tied notes within**, combine the tied notes into a single note with opposite stem direction.

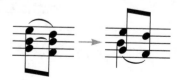

# BEGINNING OR ENDING WITH A TIE

A slur **must include both notes of the tie,** whether the tie is at the beginning or at the ending of the slur. (For an exception, see "Elisions," below.)

# ELISIONS

In keyboard music, one slur might end at the same point where another slur begins.

The two slurs **share the center of the note-head** (elide) without touching each other.

When the **elision occurs on tied notes**, the first phrase may end on the first tied note.  The second phrase can then begin on the second tied note.

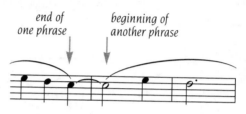

*end of*
*one phrase*

*beginning of*
*another phrase*

## GRACE-NOTE SLURS

Grace notes **may or may not have slurs.** The slurs are usually somewhat smaller to match the grace notes.

Since grace notes are always stemmed up (unless there are two voices), the slur is usually **placed below.**

Grace-note slurs may be placed more to the inside edges of the noteheads.

*grace-note slur*

*slur for beamed
grace notes*

Grace-note slurs elide with slurs.

*grace-note slurs
and slurs*

## SLURS AND ARTICULATIONS

### Beginning or ending on notes with an articulation:

The beginning or ending of a slur is placed **outside staccato and tenuto** marks.

**Center** over or under the articulation.

*slur is outside notehead and articulation*

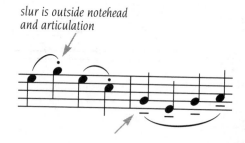

The beginning or ending of a slur is usually placed **between accents** and the notehead.

*slur is between notehead and articulation*

*here the accent is placed*
*inside the slur*

**Articulations between** the beginning and ending notes remain inside the slur.

**Fermatas** are placed **outside** the end of a slur.

## "LET RING" SLURS

The use of a short slur to indicate
continued vibration should be placed on
notes of longer duration only.  Angle the
slur slightly.

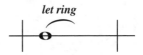

## INSTRUMENT CONSIDERATIONS

### Woodwinds and brass

Legato technique is indicated by the use of
a slur.  The slur might also indicate
breathing and phrasing.

**Slurs in combination with staccato or
tenuto marks** show varying degrees of
legato.

## For keyboards

If the space between the two staves is limited, slurs may be placed outside the staff.

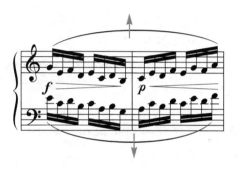

An S-shaped slur is sometimes used in music notated on the grand staff.

## For strings

Slurs can only partially indicate phrasing. Slurs are also used to indicate various bowing techniques.                    (See *Bowing*)

## For vocal music

A **slur is used for a *melisma*** (two or more notes that are to be sung on a single syllable).

The word or syllable should be placed flush left with the notehead.

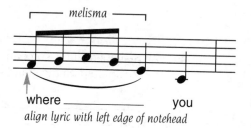

*align lyric with left edge of notehead*

Slurs to indicate phrasing in vocal music are seldom used. Since breathing is a major factor in phrasing, rests and breath marks can be used as a partial indicator of phrases.

Slurs can be drawn using a **broken line** instead of a solid one.  The broken slur is most often **used to accommodate lyrics for multiple verses.**

Similarly, **broken slurs** may also be used for syllable differences of translated text.

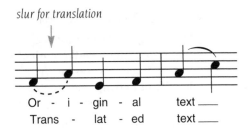

# Spacing

Spacing is of primary importance to the **visual quality** of any musical notation. While the attention to *musical* detail may be excellent, poor judgment in spacing may make the score look ill-conceived.

An awareness of spacing occurs on many levels, from the **smallest element** (the beat) **to the largest** (the score or book). The desired effect is that the notation *and* layout will immediately convey the musical intent.  Ultimately, any score should look **accessible** regardless of the level of difficulty.

## PROPORTIONAL SPACING

The concept of proportional spacing takes into consideration the **mathematical spacing** of a beat, measure and system, in relation to the **density of activity** (the number of notes per beat, measure and system).

With proportional spacing, a half note, for example, must get *more* space than a quarter note, but not *twice* as much.

## SPACING WITHIN THE MEASURE

Notes are spaced within the measure according
to a **compromise between** two extremes:

1) **Space given according to note-value** (for
example, a half note getting twice as much
space as a quarter note).

2) **Equal spacing given to each note.**

*Compare the normal (proportional) spacing with the two
extreme examples.*

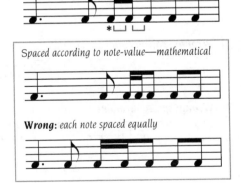

**Normal spacing**—*proportional*

Spaced according to note-value—*mathematical*

**Wrong:** *each note spaced equally*

*Make sure that consecutive notes of equal value
have equal space *following* each note.

## MEASURES WITHIN THE STAFF

The size of the measure within the staff is determined according to a **compromise between** two extremes:

1) **Equal space** for each measure.

2) Measure size **based on note density only**.

*Normal spacing of measures*

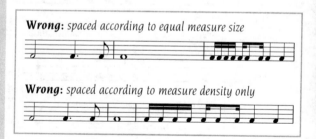

**Wrong:** *spaced according to equal measure size*

**Wrong:** *spaced according to measure density only*

## VERTICAL SPACING
### Between staves

**Musical elements** (notes on leger lines, articulations, slurs, pedal marks) **projecting beyond a staff should never conflict** with the elements of another staff or system. There should be enough space allowed for ease of reading.

### Inside systems

On the other hand, the **staves of a system should not be too far apart.** This is especially important for a system that is to be read by one performer—a keyboard player, for example. The eye should not have to jump too far from one staff to the other, in order to read notes for the right and left hand simultaneously.

*The most common misjudgment is to place staves (or systems) exactly the same distance from one another without adjusting to compensate for the projecting musical elements.*

### Between systems

**More space should be be provided between systems** than between the *staves* of the systems.

The **spacing between systems should be balanced,** with the page margins and the number of systems on the page in mind.  If the **page is dense,** the systems will be closer to each other and to the minimum vertical margins, while allowing enough distance between systems to distinguish one from another.  If the **page is sparse,** the upper and lower page margins could be larger.

## GENERAL PAGE LAYOUT
### Page numbers

**The position of the page number in relation to the page edges should *never* change, regardless of page spacing.**  Printers can use the page number as a guide for positioning the image area on the page.

If page numbers are placed to the left and right, as is usual, **even numbers** are always to the **left, odd numbers** always to the **right.**  Page numbers may be centered, but this is not the usual practice. Centered page numbers interfere more with the music and text.

Page numbers should be positioned **no closer than 1/4 inch from** the top (or bottom) of the **page edge**.

## Title page

The title, credits, copyright and any accompanying text can be **vertically adjusted to accommodate** a loosely spaced page or a tightly spaced page. Such type should always be well placed, considering the space allowed.

## Facing pages

Facing pages **should look good together.** As much as possible, they should have a **balanced look** (notes on a system, number of systems, white space, etc.). The vertical page margins should be the same if at all possible.

## Page turns

It is very important to lay out the measures and systems in a manner that will allow a good page turn. Having **rests in the last measure** before the page turn is the most desirable. Second to rests would be perhaps a whole note (that could be held with the pedal) or a sparse measure—anything that would allow a hand to be free to turn the page.

Try to **minimize the number of page turns** by adjusting the amount of music on the page or by changing the sequence of pieces.

## Book layout

Calculating the number of pages needed or what will work in the allowed number of pages is crucial to an appealing layout.

If a book contains many short pieces and a particular order is not important (or can be adjusted slightly), there are several things that can be done to make a good layout.

Often a piece can be **condensed or expanded** to offer choice page turns and good facing pages.

Consider reordering the pieces to **minimize the number of page turns. Group pieces** with an odd number of pages together so that the ones with an even number of pages can have facing pages.

A poorly placed piece at the beginning of a book can throw off the facing pages for the rest of the book.

## Backing up

Expect to go back and **adjust various elements** (page turns, systems, staves, measures or notes within a measure) when planning a layout for a book. A change in the order of pieces and the number of pages might create density problems on other pages.

> *The part must be considered with the whole and the whole considered with the part.*

## White space

With experience comes the **appreciation of white space** on a page or within a book. There is nothing more daunting than overwhelming density. The eye should be guided from note to note, measure to measure, staff to staff and page to page with a minimum of surprises. If a performer must stop playing in order to understand the notation, or loses his place because of poor placement, the notation and layout are *not* successful.

# Staccato                                    see *Articulations*

# *Staff*

The staff commonly consists of five lines.

The **staff line weight** should be thick
enough to be clearly legible but thin
enough for the notes of the staff to be
easily read.

A staff line will be **thicker than stem lines**
and **equal to** (or thinner than) **barlines.**

If a note is on the line, the line will always
run through the **center of the notehead,**
regardless of the note value.

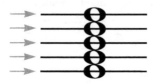

**A notehead in a space** is always clearly positioned between the two staff lines.

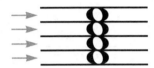

A **one-line staff** is used for non-pitched percussion.

or

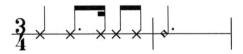

**Leger lines** extend the range of the staff.

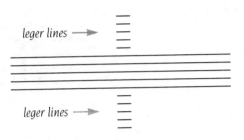

leger lines →

leger lines →

**Barlines** divide the staff into measures.

A **clef** placed on a five-line staff determines the pitches for each line and space.

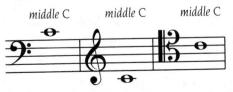

middle C     middle C     middle C

A **key signature** determines the key of the music notated on the staff.

Two or more staves grouped together (with a systemic barline) form a **system.**

A **bracket** groups staves into systems or parts of systems.          (See Bracket)

A **brace** groups staves into a **grand staff.**          (See Brace)

*Some examples of systems:*

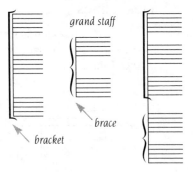

*grand staff*

*brace*

*bracket*

The **first system** (or staff) of music is usually **indented** about 1/2 inch.

# *Stems*

Stems are **thinner than staff lines and barlines.**

STEM LENGTH

The **normal stem length** is $3^1/_2$ spaces (one octave).

*one octave*

## With leger lines

When a note extends **beyond one leger line,** the stem **must touch the middle staff line.**

## When parts share a staff

Up-stem notes **above the middle line are shorter** than normal. Traditionally, their stem length is relative to surrounding notes, getting progressively shorter as the notes go higher. The shortest stem length is 2½ spaces (interval of a 6th).

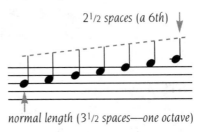

*2½ spaces (a 6th)*

*normal length (3½ spaces—one octave)*

*For the computer, a setting should be chosen that works well for most situations.*

Down-stem notes **below the middle line** follow the same guidelines as the above.

## With the interval of a 2nd

The stem is always placed **between the two notes** of an interval of a 2nd, with the **upper note always to the right,** the **lower note always to the left.**

## STEM DIRECTION

For notes on the **middle line and above,** the stem is down.

For notes **below the middle line,** the stem is up.

## When sharing a staff

Notes have **opposite stem direction** when sharing a staff. (Stems in the "wrong direction" will have shorter stems, as previously mentioned.)

## When notes share a stem

If the **note above is farther** from the middle line than the note below, the **stem goes down.**

If the note **below is farther** from the middle line, the **stem goes up.**

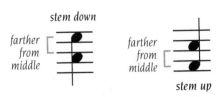

When the two notes are an **equal distance from the middle line,** the preferred direction is down.

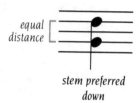

*stem preferred down*

If a **pattern of stem direction** is established, stem direction is *sometimes* maintained when the notes are an equal distance from the middle. (This practice is all but obsolete.)

The same rules apply to *more than two notes* sharing a stem. The **distance of the OUTER NOTES from the middle line** determines stem direction.

When the **outer notes** are an **equal distance from the middle line** and the majority of notes are above the middle line, the stem goes down.

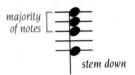

*majority of notes*   *stem down*

When the **outer notes** are an **equal distance from the middle line** and the majority of notes are below the middle line, the stem goes up.

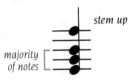

*stem up*   *majority of notes*

## For beamed groups

Simple rules for stemming of single notes and chords apply to beamed groups when possible (for example, if all notes in a beamed grouping are on or above the middle line of the staff, stems are down).

(See *Beams*)

# Systems

Two or more staves grouped together
(with a systemic barline) form a system.

A **bracket** groups staves into systems or
parts of systems.                    (See Bracket)

A **brace** groups staves into a **grand staff.**
                    (See Brace and Grand staff)

*Some examples of systems:*

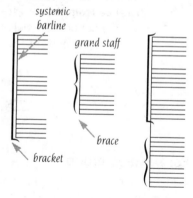

(See Barlines)

The **first system** of music is usually
**indented** about 1/2 inch.

# Tablature

Tablature is a system of notation that graphically represents the strings and frets of a stringed instrument (such as guitar).

The letters **"TAB"** are placed where a clef would normally be. The only function of these letters is to identify the staff as being tablature.

Each note is indicated by **placing the fret number on the appropriate string.**

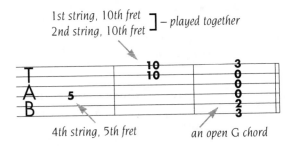

1st string, 10th fret
2nd string, 10th fret ] – *played together*

4th string, 5th fret          *an open G chord*

Tablature does NOT indicate rhythmic values; therefore, a five-line staff using **standard notation** is placed above the tablature staff.

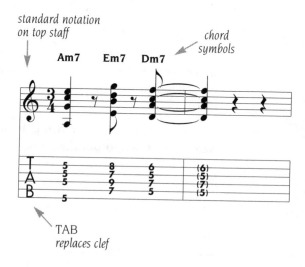

*standard notation on top staff*

*chord symbols*

TAB *replaces clef*

A **systemic barline connects** the two staves together.  Measure **barlines** are broken.

**Chord symbols** (when appropriate) are often added above the top staff.

**Picking or fingering techniques** notated on the top staff are repeated on the tablature staff.

Every note on the top staff must have a **corresponding finger number** on the tablature staff—**tied notes** are in parentheses.

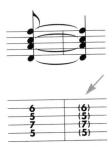

Tablature may consist of **four lines** (for electric bass and mandolin) or **five lines** (five-string banjo).

The **notation** for guitar tablature outlined on the previous pages applies to all tablature, regardless of the number of strings.

### Electric bass

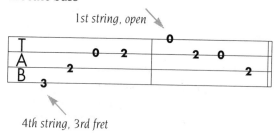

*1st string, open*

*4th string, 3rd fret*

### Five-string banjo

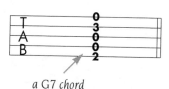

*a G7 chord*

# *Tempo marks*

Tempo marks indicating the rate of speed may be followed by an expression mark and/or metronome mark.

The left edge of the tempo mark is **vertically aligned to the left edge of the time signature.**

*The type is bold Roman.*

## WITH EXPRESSION MARKS

Tempo marks are often accompanied by an indication of **expression;** however, expression marks should **never** *replace* tempo marks.

**Presto con brio**

**Slowly, with much emotion**

## WITH METRONOME MARKS

The tempo mark may be more precisely indicated with the addition of a metronome mark.

The metronome mark may be **specific,** a tempo **range** or **general.**  The type is slightly smaller than that of the tempo and is usually enclosed in parentheses.  The note is cue size or smaller.

**Allegro con moto** ( ♩ = 144)

**Allegro con moto** ( ♩ = 132–144)

**Allegro con moto** ( ♩ = ca. 144)

## TEMPO VARIATIONS

If the tempo is *varied* by the use of markings such as **ritardando, rallentando** or **accelerando,** the term **a tempo** is placed at the point where the tempo is reinstated. Unlike the usual placement of tempo variations, **a tempo** is often indicated above the staff. *The type will be bold italic.*

If the tempo is *changed,* and then returns to the original tempo later in the piece, the term **Tempo I** is indicated **above the staff.** *The type will be bold Roman.*

# Tenuto

*See Articulations*

# Ties

A tie connects **two consecutive notes of the same pitch,** extending the duration of the first note to include the second.  (The second note does not have its own attack.)

> The shape of a tie is somewhat similar to a slur, but the **placement, positioning and use of ties and slurs are different;** the two should not be confused.

## BEGINNING AND ENDING

**Begin and end on the same horizontal level.**

**Begin to the right** of the notehead.
**End to the left** of the next notehead.
The tie **does not touch the noteheads.**

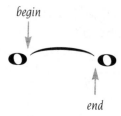

## AVOID AUGMENTATION DOTS

Ties should never collide with augmentation dots. **Begin the tie to the right of an augmentation dot.**

## PLACEMENT ON THE STAFF

### Avoid touching staff lines.

Place the **center** of the curve in a "space."

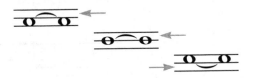

### Ends of ties may cross staff lines—it is
better to cross even slightly, than to just
touch a staff line.

### Adjust curve for longer ties.

Raise or lower the center of the curve to
the next space.

## DIRECTION ON THE STAFF

**Curve ties opposite of stem direction.**
Stem down—curve above notehead.
Stem up—curve below notehead.

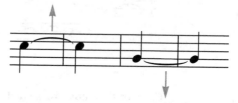

**Ties on whole notes** are treated as if the whole notes had stems.

**For mixed stem direction,** the tie is always placed **above.**

## SHARING THE SAME STAFF

For two parts, place ties **above for the upper part, below for the lower part.**

For two *sets* of parts, place ties **above for the upper two parts, below for the lower two parts.**

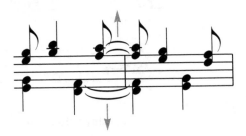

## MULTIPLE TIED NOTES

**When more than two notes are tied,** ties must be added from note to note.

## WRAPPING FROM STAFF TO STAFF

**Align end** of tie with end of staff.

**Continue tie in the lower staff** immediately after the key signature (or clef).

Beginning and ending points always
remain on the **same horizontal level**.

## DIRECTION OF TIES FOR CHORDS

**Highest** note—tie is **above**.

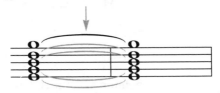

**Lowest** note—tie is **below**.

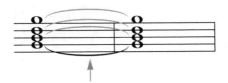

Notes between highest and lowest—on the
**middle line and above**, ties are **above**.

**Below** the **middle line**, ties are **below**.

For **intervals of a 2nd**, ties will be in
**opposite directions** whenever possible.

**If some notes are not tied** within the chords, the uppermost tied note has the tie above; the lowermost tied note has the tie below.

*top tie up*

*bottom tie down*

## ALIGNMENT OF TIE ENDS

**Align ends of ties** within a chord.

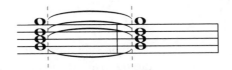

**Tie ends for intervals of a 2nd** should be adjusted if possible.

## ADJUSTMENT OF TIES

Whenever possible, **maintain the curve** of a tie in uncommon situations. It should look like a tie, not a slur.

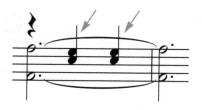

*In this instance it is better to have the top tie curved up even though it is a part of the lower voice.*

**If a time signature interrupts a tie, break the tie** to avoid colliding with the time signature.

## BROKEN (DASHED) TIES

Ties using a broken line instead of a solid one are often **used to accommodate lyrics for multiple verses.**

When will you be there for
No - where have I seen

## TIES IN MEASURED ARPEGGIOS

Although traditionally considered incorrect, ties are sometimes **extended to the unbroken chord** to avoid a cluttered look.

*Traditional*

# Time signatures

Time signatures indicate the meter for a measure(s) or an entire piece.

Since meter is so closely connected with the proper use of ties, rests, beams and syncopated rhythms, the **correct time signature** must be chosen.

> The **upper number** indicates the number of beats per measure.
>
> The **lower number** indicates the note that gets one beat (2 = half note, 4 = quarter note, 8 = eighth note, 16 = sixteenth note, etc.).

All measures after a time signature will be in the same meter until a new time signature is indicated.

## PLACEMENT

> The **upper number** is always placed between the top line and the middle line of the staff.

The **lower number** is always placed between the middle line and the bottom line of the staff.

For a **single-line staff,** the line intersects the two numbers.

The time signature is **indicated after the clef and key signature.**

## CHANGING TIME SIGNATURES

Time signatures may change from measure to measure, applying to all measures until the next time signature change. **A change in time signature always appears AFTER a barline.**

If the time signature changes at the beginning of a line, a **courtesy time signature** is added at the end of the previous staff, *after* the last barline. The new time signature appears after the clef (and key signature, if any) on the next staff.

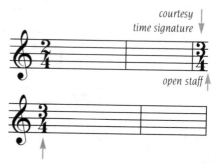

*courtesy time signature*

*open staff*

The following illustrates the positioning of the clef, key signature and time signature if all three change simultaneously.

(*double barline is added for key signature change*)

**COMPOSITE METER**            (See Meter)
**ALTERNATING METER**          (See Meter)

# *Tremolo*

A tremolo may be **on one note,** or **between two or more notes.** It may be **measured** (a clear subdivision) or **unmeasured** (as fast as possible).

## ON ONE NOTE
### Measured tremolo

A **short slanted line,** ascending from left to right, through the stem of a note indicates that a note is to be subdivided.

Each line placed on the stem indicates the **rhythmic value** of the tremolo.

*For instance, one line will indicate eighth notes, two lines—sixteenth notes.*

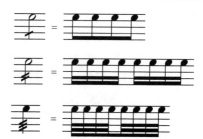

In string music, a measured tremolo is sometimes indicated by placing **divisi dots** above the note, in addition to the slashes through the stem.

The divisi dots precisely indicate the divisions per note. The slashes through the stem indicate the rhythmic value.

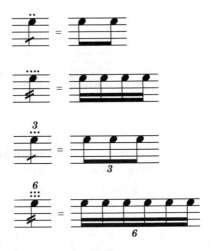

## Unmeasured tremolo

An **unmeasured tremolo** (on one note) is indicated by placing three lines through the stem and adding the abbreviation ***trem.*** above the note. (If placed on a beamed note, the beam counts as one of the lines.) Most often seen in notation for strings, percussion and fretted instruments.

Tremolo lines on whole notes are traditionally **indicated above or below the note** (positioned as if there were a stem, but centered on the notehead).

*traditional style*

**Modern style** breaks the whole note into two half notes and places the slanted lines through the stems as usual.

*modern style*

## ON MORE THAN ONE NOTE

When a tremolo is indicated between two (or more) different pitches, the notes are connected with a beam, with incomplete beams placed between to indicate the rhythmic value.

*Stems are lengthened to accommodate added beams.*

With such a subdivision of the tremolo, **each note equals the total rhythmic value of the tremolo.**

*unmeasured whole-note tremolo (traditional style)*

*modern style*

In the previous example, a complete measure of tremolo in $\frac{4}{4}$ time consists of two sets of half notes beamed together.

## INTERVAL / CHORD TREMOLO

For some instruments, a tremolo is possible between two, three or more notes.

# *Trill*

The abbreviation *tr* indicates a trill.

The *tr* is always **placed above the note**, regardless of stem direction (unless two parts share a staff).

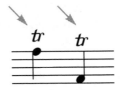

**Each trilled note** must have its own trill symbol.

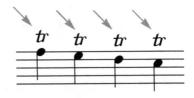

A **wavy line** may be indicated after the **tr**, especially if the trill is extended.

If the trill **extends over two or more notes,** the wavy line continues to the end of the notehead of the last note affected by the trill.

*end just after notehead*

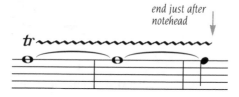

If the **wavy line extends over consecutive notes of the same pitch** but without ties, the notes are to be clearly articulated.

**When two parts share a staff**, the trill for the lower part is placed below the note.

When the upper note of a trill is **altered from the diatonic scale**, a small **accidental** is used with the trill sign. The accidental is placed after the trill sign but before the wavy line (if used.)

The accidental **may also appear above** the trill sign.

A **cue-size notehead** is sometimes used.

**Terminations** can be indicated by cue-size or full-size notes.

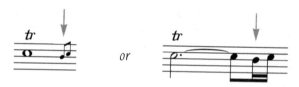

*played:*

*termination*

# Triplet

See *Tuplets*

# *Tuplets*

Rhythmic groupings of notes that are NOT metric groupings are known as **tuplets.**

*Duplets, triplets, quadruplets, quintuplets, sextuplets and septuplets are all examples of* **tuplets.**

## TUPLET NUMERALS

The numeral is larger than a finger number and is **distinctly italic, preferably bold italic.**    (See *Fingerings [for keyboard]*)

For beamed tuplets, the numeral is preferred **on the beam side, centered.**

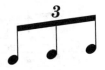

*Do not use a tuplet slur with the numeral. This is an obsolete practice and causes confusion between normal slurs and tuplet slurs.*

Place the tuplet numeral **outside the staff** whenever possible.

> If placed within the staff, the **numeral must be clearly positioned,** avoiding staff lines as much as possible.
>
> The numeral **remains placed with the beam,** whatever the stem direction.

**When parts share a staff,** the numeral is placed normally (beam/stem side).

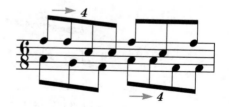

After a **pattern of tuplets** has been
established, the numeral may be omitted.
*Simile* may also be used for clarity.

## TUPLET BRACKETS

If the tuplet is not beamed, a **bracket is
added** and the **numeral is centered**
within the bracket.

The bracket always **begins flush left** with
the notehead and **ends flush right** with
the notehead, whether on the notehead or
stem side.

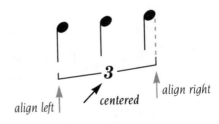

The **bracket is broken** to accommodate the number; the **ends** are always vertical.

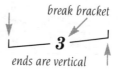

*break bracket*

*ends are vertical*

If the tuplet numeral is **moved to the notehead side** of a beamed tuplet (for example, to avoid fingerings), add a bracket for clarity.

The **bracket is placed** at the same angle as the beam.

*angle identical to beam*

When placing a **bracket with unbeamed notes,** the bracket angle can vary.

## BRACKETS AND UNEQUAL VALUES

For **unequal rhythmic values** within the tuplet group, the bracket must **include all notes** of the group.

The **numeral remains centered** within the bracket.

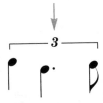

The tuplet unit is clearly seen if the bracket extends to **include the entire allotted space** for the tuplet (as in the first tuplet below).

*The bracket does not extend to include the flag (as shown in the second tuplet).*

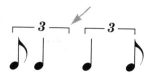

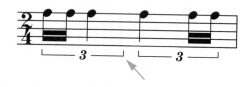

## WITH RESTS

The **bracket extends** to include rests.

Although the bracket is preferred, an option is to **extend the beam** to include the rest within the tuplet.

## WITH FINGERINGS

It is advised to **move the tuplet figure to avoid confusion with finger numbers.**

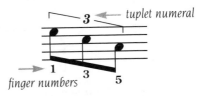

## WITH ARTICULATIONS

If the bracket must be placed on the same side as articulations, the bracket is **placed outside articulations.**

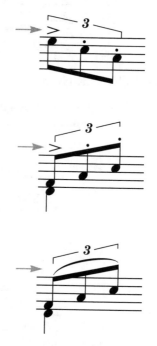

*Short slurs may be considered articulations.*

## DETERMINING NOTE VALUE

A tuplet may occupy a beat, a pulse, a *portion* of a beat or pulse, or an entire measure.

To determine the rhythmic value of a tuplet that occupies **one beat,** subdivide the beat metrically as many times as you can without exceeding the number of notes in the tuplet. The note value of the tuplet will be equal to the note value of that metric subdivision.

*In the example below, if each beat were subdivided further, it would have more notes than the tuplet; therefore the tuplet notes are sixteenth notes.*

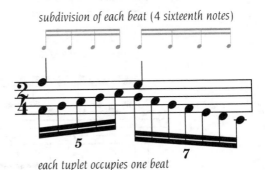

*subdivision of each beat (4 sixteenth notes)*

*each tuplet occupies one beat*

Use the same principle to determine the note value of tuplets that occupy an **entire measure** (or another unit of a measure).

*subdivision of the measure (4 eighth notes)*

*tuplets occupying an entire measure*

*subdivision of the measure (12 sixteenth notes)*

*tuplets occupying an entire measure*

**Duplets are the only exception** to the previous rule deciding tuplet rhythmic value.

> Duplets are **equal in rhythmic value to the beat** (not to be confused with pulse).
>
> Duplets only occur in **compound meter**.

*subdivision of the* PULSE
*(3 eighth notes)*

Duplets

## HORIZONTAL SPACING

> A tuplet is spaced mathematically, as proper spacing dictates—not aligned with the metric rhythm.

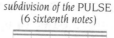

*subdivision of the PULSE*
*(6 sixteenth notes)*

*tuplet occupying one pulse*
*(entire measure)*

## COURTESY TUPLET NUMERALS

When a piece has many tuplets, numerals are sometimes used to clarify groupings that are regular to the meter.

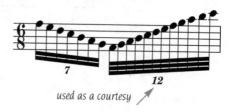

*used as a courtesy*

However, the **12** would be unnecessary if the secondary beams were divided between beats (see Beams).

# Volti subito

*Volti* means to turn the page.

***Volti subito (v.s.)*** would indicate to turn the page *quickly*.

> *Volti subito* alerts the performer to turn the page quickly in order to avoid unnecessary surprise on the following page.
>
> **Place below the staff** and at the most logical location, usually the **last measure of the page.** Allow sufficient time (rests) to prepare for the page turn whenever possible.

# Words                                    *See Lyric*

# X *notehead*                        *See Notes*

# Index of Topics